3692

Baroque Music:
Style and Performance

BAROQUE MUSIC: STYLE AND PERFORMANCE

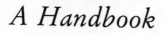

A Handbook

ROBERT DONINGTON

W · W · NORTON & COMPANY

NEW YORK · LONDON

ISBN 0-393-30052-8

Printed in Great Britain

Contents

─────

Contents

Tables

―――――

Author's Note

This handbook follows three earlier books of mine concerned with baroque music and its interpretation.

The first to be published was *The Interpretation of Early Music* (1963), in which I brought together as much contemporary evidence as I could then find in support of a very full discussion both of the principles and of the details of interpretation, mainly for the baroque period. Large as it was, this became nearly half as large again when *The Interpretation of Early Music: New Version* was issued in 1974. The second, *A Performer's Guide to Baroque Music* (1973), was designed to be more compact and utilitarian, though it also goes more fully into certain topics. The scope of the third book, *String Playing in Baroque Music* (1977), was more specific, being primarily to interest general rather than specializing string players in many crucial points of baroque style and technique.

The present book has in view the needs of students, performers and others for a basic grounding. It summarizes the principles of authentic interpretation in baroque music and their practical application in performance. It deliberately leaves out the more complicated or controversial refinements, but it brings in whatever I should now regard as essential, substantiated by the evidence of the baroque composers and writers themselves. Not every reader, I hope, will take this evidence in quite the same way, for baroque music was never meant to be taken in quite the same way, and we shall not succeed today by being rigid and impersonal. But in providing the basic information, I hope to have given readers the means by which their own understanding and interpretation of the music may fall within the broad boundaries of baroque style and performance.

Robert Donington
Firle, Sussex
October 1981

Chapter One · Getting the Feel

Style and performance in baroque music present certain problems due not only to neglect but also to misguided enthusiasms at various periods on the way down. Romantic exaggerations have tended to be over-compensated by austere understatements no nearer to the spirit of the originals and considerably more inhibiting to our musicianly enjoyment. Our aim today is for a more authentic balance. There are so many practical decisions which can be taken better in the light of whatever evidence survives about how the original performers took them when the music was contemporary and its interpretation a matter of relatively common knowledge.

This book rests on direct quotations from contemporary sources, bibliographical references for which will be found at the end, listed by number, and also alphabetically by authors' names. My running commentary will draw the material together as best I can; but the evidence comes first. There are, of course, inevitably gaps and inconsistencies, but this broadly is how the story goes. I shall start it with a general point about warmth of feeling, and then go on to some of the particularities which make the baroque applications of it so often different from our own.

(1) *Sir Thomas More, Louvain, 1516 (in English, London, 1551):* Music among the admired Utopians 'dothe so resemble and expresse natural affections, the sound and tune is so applied and made agreeable to the thinge, that whether it bee a prayer, or els a dytty of gladnes, of patience, of trouble, of mournynge, or of anger: the fassion of the melodye doethe so represent the meaning of the thing, that it doth wonderfully move, stirre, pearce, and enflame the hearers myndes'.

(2) *Baldassare Castiglione, Venice, 1528 (in English, 1561):* Music will 'recreate a man, but for sundrie causes, as a man may perceive in the manner of singing that Bido useth, which is so artificall, cunning, vehement, stirred, and such sundrie melodies, that the spirites of the hearers move all and are inflamed, and so listing, a man would weene they were lift up into heaven. And no lesse doth our Marchetto Cara move in his singing, but with a more soft harmony, that by a

delectable way and full of mourning sweetenes maketh tender and perceth the mind, and sweetly imprinteth in it a passion full of great delite.'

(3) Richard Hooker, London, 1597: 'An admirable faculty which music hath to express and represent to the mind more inwardly than any other sensible mean, the very standing, rising, and falling, the very steps and inflections every way, the turns and varieties of all passions whereunto the mind is subject.'

(4) Charles Butler, London, 1636: Music, 'having a great power over the affections of the mind', requires the composer to be 'transported as it were with some Musical fury; so that himself scarce knoweth what he doth, nor can presently give a reason for his doing'.

(5) Sir Thomas Browne, London, 1642: 'There is a musick where ever there is a harmony, order or proportion'; thus 'even that vulgar and Tavern-Musick which makes one man merry, another mad, strikes in me a deep fit of devotion, and a profound contemplation of the First Composer. There is something in it of Divinity more than the ear discovers: it is an Hieroglyphical and shadowed lesson of the whole World, and creatures of God; such a melody to the ear, as the whole World, well understood, would afford the understanding.'

(6) Thomas Mace, London, 1676: 'That Vast-Conchording-Unity of the whole *Congregational Chorus,* came (as I may say) *Thundering in,* even so, as it made the very *Ground shake* under us; *(Oh the unutterable ravishing Soul's delight!)* In the which I was so *transported,* and *wrapt* up into *High Contemplations,* that there was no room left in my *whole Man,* viz. *Body, Soul* and *Spirit,* for any thing below *Divine* and *Heavenly Raptures.'* For 'in Musick, may any *Humour, Conceit,* or *Passion* (never so various) be Exprest'.

(7) Angelo Berardi, Bologna, 1681: 'Music is the ruler of the passions of the soul.'

(8) François Raguenet, Paris, 1702 (Eng. trans., 1709): Music is 'transport, enchantment and extasy of pleasure'.

(9) François Couperin, Paris, 1716: 'I declare in all good faith that I am more pleased with what moves me than with what astonishes me.'

(10) Johann David Heinichen, Dresden, 1728: the 'true aim of music' is 'to move the feelings'.

(11) Francesco Geminiani, London, 1749: the performer will do justice to the composer 'if while his Imagination is warm and glowing he pours the same exalted Spirit into his own Performance'.

(12) Friedrich Wilhelm Marpurg, Berlin, 1749: 'All musical expression has an affect or emotion for its foundation', demanding 'the utmost sensibility and the most felicitous powers of intuition'.

(13) Joachim Quantz, 1752: 'The composer and he who performs the music must alike have a feeling soul, and one capable of being moved.'

(14) C. P. E. Bach, 1753: 'A musician cannot move others unless he too is moved.'

A variety of idioms

The above quotations confirm that a normal range of human feelings is to be expected in baroque music; but the variety of idioms and of moods within this long period is of course very great indeed. Both history and geography must be taken into consideration, since each time and place had its own styles and practices, and inferences drawn from one to another can be very hazardous.

As an example, the treatises cited above by Quantz and by C. P. E. Bach are the most thorough and extensive we possess from the middle of the eighteenth century, and for areas under the general influence of France and the particular influence of Berlin. How far back can we apply them safely, and how widely? Well, J. S. Bach was in much of his music under that French influence, which had been going on in Germany for over half a century when those books were written. True, it was a time of crucial transition, but J. S. Bach himself took a hand with that in his own 'galant' music. Quantz was born only twelve years later than J. S. Bach, and had the same background and training, besides having a taste which Dr Burney *(15)* in 1773 called 'that of forty years ago'. C. P. E. Bach was trained by his father, whom he praised more for his pioneering than for his conservative qualities, and whom he resembled in some though not all of his music (his big fantasias, for example). There is indeed a generation gap, and we must be careful; but there is also much to be learned about the first half of the eighteenth century from these two writers who stood so much closer to J. S. Bach than we do ourselves. We need not only an awareness of history and geography but a keen sense of musical appropriateness in applying any musicological evidence to any music. If it does not end up sounding musicianly it is not acceptable musicologically, and we must think again. But we still need to go on making the best we can of the evidence.

We may next consider the most radical distinction of nationality for all periods of baroque music, and one which persisted on much the same lines throughout. Its general importance for our understanding and our interpretations alike will not be overlooked.

(16) Marin Mersenne, Paris, 1636–7: The Italians 'represent as much as they can the passions and the affects of the soul and the spirit', whereas 'our Frenchmen are content to caress the ear, and use nothing but a perpetual sweetness'.

(17) Georg Muffat, Augsburg, 1695: The French style [as learned by Muffat under Lully] has 'natural melody with an easy, and smooth line, quite devoid of superfluous, extravagant ornamental improvisations'.

(18) François Raguenet, Paris, 1702 (in English, 1709): 'The French, in their airs, aim at the soft, the easy, the flowing and the coherent', whereas 'the Italians venture at everything that is harsh and out of the way'; for 'as the Italians are naturally much more brisk than the French, so they are more sensible of the passions'; though it must be admitted that in France, they play 'much finer and with a greater nicety'.

(19) Roger North (undated, but in London around the turn of the seventeenth and eighteenth centuries, reminiscing): The court [of Charles II] 'entertained only the theatrical music and French air in song, but that somewhat softened and variegated', until 'the time came off the French way and fell in with the Italian, and now that holds the ear. But still the English singularity will come in and have a share.'

(20) Pier Francesco Tosi, Bologna, 1723 (Eng. trans., 1742): [regardless of nationality] 'for the theatre' the performance should be 'lively and various; for the chamber, delicate and finish'd; and for the Church moving and grave'. But unfortunately, 'this difference, to many *Moderns*, is quite unknown'.

(21) Johann David Heinichen, Dresden, 1728 [another view, but very relevant, for example, to J. S. Bach]: 'Practical modern musicians are rightly inclined to depart from the unseasoned character of a too antique church style.'

(22) Joachim Quantz, Berlin, 1752: 'After the pupil has gained also a general idea of the differences of taste in music, he must recognise distinctive pieces of different nations and provinces, and learn to play them each according to its kind.' Thus 'Italian music is less restrained than any other; but the French is almost too much so, whence it comes about perhaps that in French music the new always seems like the old. Nevertheless the French method of playing is not at all to be despised, above all an apprentice should be recommended to mix the propriety and the clarity of the French with the light and shade of the Italian instrumentalists.' The leading nations in music are 'the Italians and the French. Other nations are ruled in their taste

by these two.' [But everywhere] 'Church music requires a grander and more serious manner than theatre music, and this last allows more liberty.' [However] 'Almost every musician has a different expression from that of others. It is not only the different teaching that they have received which causes this variety; the difference of temperament and character also contributes'; for 'the diversity of taste depends upon the diversity of temperaments'. [And finally and very aptly] 'One is not always in the same mood'.

It is valuable to be reminded in this manner that personality and temperament are legitimate variables. We should never assume that there can only be one right and authentic way: that never was and is not now the case. Flexibility is of the essence of good baroque interpretation.

Chapter Two · Preparing the Text

One of the most striking features which gives its characteristic quality to baroque music is the freedom it grants to the performer in improvising the greater part of the expression as he goes along, and even quite a substantial part of the notes. Nothing is regarded as entirely fixed. Everything is just that much open to the mood of the moment. It is possible to be inconsistent, wayward, imaginative and unpredictable, and if you are sufficiently in touch with the style of your piece, no harm need come of it, but rather all the enjoyment of a spontaneous liberty within bounds. No wonder baroque music appeals strongly to our freedom-loving generation. Much of our own contemporary music pursues just such spontaneity, and in baroque music this ingredient is contained in the very conditions of its authentic performance.

Nevertheless, there is the responsibility attaching to this freedom. It is necessary to know the style, and to respect the conventions which set outer boundaries to it. The secret of baroque musicianship is imagination and fantasy within the boundaries of style. To interpret the music it is necessary not only to understand the music but to know the conventions. The reason for this is that these conventions were never set there to be arbitrary limitations. On the contrary, they evolved in course of the creative process: they are themselves aspects of the creative process. We shall learn them again as much by empathy as by instruction, but all the same we have to learn them, and learn them well, before we can really begin to follow the baroque example of leaving our interpretations almost entirely to be worked out in rehearsal and performance.

There is some very good baroque-style rehearsing and improvising and performing going on now, and our best choice of method is very largely a matter of degree. Yet the fact remains that the open quality so characteristic both of the spirit and the performance of baroque music sets a challenge which has to be very fully met if our methods are to succeed. Indeed, the farther back into history, the less responsibility taken by composers, and the more left to interpreters. Not till the nineteenth century were notated scores meant to finalize as much as possible. Baroque scores, in a sense, are incomplete: we might say that they are deliberately incomplete. An awful lot of editing has got to happen somewhere along the line before the music can glow out at us in all its intended clarity and glory. It can be written editing, or it can be mental editing, or it can be some of each; but under present conditions, rapidly as they are expanding, paper-work ahead of rehearsal is almost always an essential part of the preparation. What comes up spontaneously in rehearsal may be better still, but the chances are that if it has not been well prepared it will not be well done. There is work to be put in on the score and the parts before ever they are set out on the music stands.

In all this we shall do well not to forget that the virtue of the baroque approach is to encourage and not to hamper our spontaneity. How much to write down, how much to improvise, how much more or less to memorize depends on circumstances. Orchestral parts need more marking up as a rule than chamber parts, where discussion during rehearsal is more feasible (though always best when least is put into words and most is done at the point of the bow and the rest). In general, too little editing risks ending up with a rendering neither quite one thing nor quite another, and rather more hesitant than can carry full conviction; too much editing annoys experienced performers and hinders them from bringing their own informed imagination freely to bear. No existing edition, in any case, need be treated with undue respect: it is only one man's sample working. 'Be your own editor' comes much nearer to the baroque situation. That is what the baroque composer expected and deserves, not an excess of misplaced nineteenth-century textual reverence.

But in one way or another the editing must get done, or the music suffers. Careful preparation by the director of an ensemble, perhaps in consultation, but certainly before actual rehearsing begins, is likely to save time and trouble and to make for well-defined performances; much of this careful preparation, though by no means all, is likely to repay marking into the score and parts.

Acquiring the material

The most radical way of acquiring baroque material is to seek it out in the great libraries possessing holdings of early prints and manuscripts. Fresh discoveries can be made, though for public performance a high standard of selection is desirable. Mere novelty or mere historic interest does not satisfy an audience, and items of marginal value as music should ordinarily be kept for private consumption.

Most great libraries admit by ticket on the recommendation of a reputable sponsor. Catalogues of their holdings may usually be consulted in print, so as to avoid vain journeys or waste of precious opening hours. A research scholar may need to examine the paper, the ink, the watermarks – the physical characteristics of the source; otherwise, a microfilm or photocopy will serve, or a facsimile edition if one is available. Photocopying can generally be arranged if the call number and page or folio numbers are supplied.

Some sources are unique, and then the text must be taken as it comes. Other texts survive in variant copies or states from which the best version (not always the earliest) can be chosen or pieced together. This can sometimes be done from a good and scholarly printed edition in which a modern editor has been at pains to indicate any variants of musical significance, and to make it plain by typographical distinctions or other indications just what is in the original and what he has editorially added or changed. There are in practice typographical limits to the degree of completeness and clearness with which this can be done; but mere silent editing is a serious defect in scholarly editions, though in performing editions it is normal and acceptable. Performers as such do not want to be distracted by too many fine distinctions, which can interfere with legibility and pass on to them more responsibility for detailed decisions on the text and the interpretation than they may wish to take.

Editions under the promising title *Urtext* (Ger., 'original text') may give an excellent modern transcription, so long as it is appreciated that transcription is already editing, since it involves many decisions about how to represent the original notation in modern equivalents. If variant sources survive, further decisions are needed about which source to use, or what combination of sources, until we may find ourselves asking in the end what is meant by original. A facsimile is the only full reproduction of an original text, and this may be quite hard to sight-read although invaluable to study.

Any modern edition in which the unavoidable decisions and changes and additions have been moderate and sensible may serve very well, especially if it is of a form increasingly employed, in which the most necessary scholarly information is combined with clear legibility and sufficient editorial assistance: a combined-purpose edition. It is always possible to add or alter phrasing and dynamic markings, to thin down or fill out continuo realizations, and in other ways make over the editing to individual preference. A modern edition with not too much black ink on the page will leave more room for these personal markings, best done in pencil to allow for further thoughts.

Modern editions vary enormously in quality, and it is often an open question whether to adapt one in this way or to start a clean manuscript of one's own; or of course there may be no modern edition, and starting fresh is then the only method. Making an edition is very laborious, but with early music it is a frequent necessity, and can be very rewarding, including as it may do a considerable element of subsidiary composing. For one part of baroque editing lies in completing the notes; another part lies in outlining the expression.

Completing the notes

There will often be a continuo consisting of a bass line on which an accompaniment has to be realized with the help of any figures which may be given (figured bass). This can be done more or less at sight, which was the normal baroque expectation and gives much the most spontaneous and natural effect when it is really well done: but some preparation at the keyboard, if opportunity arises, helps marvellously and was commonly recommended; and, of course, a realization once performed can be partly written out or memorized, and partly improved in subsequent performances, until it grows to be something of a vintage product. The skill to do this is in fact basic to baroque interpretation, and is being increasingly taught and practised. But since it is not by any means in every accompanist's possession as yet, editors usually (and I think rightly) supply for publication a realization fully worked out in writing. This can be used as it stands; or thinned out if it is too heavy and pianistic in the old-fashioned manner; or enriched with further figuration or voice-leading if it is too sparse and self-denying in one fairly common modern fashion.

Some editors prefer to challenge the performer by supplying only the bass and figures, but it seems more practical to include a sample working for those who need it. It can be kept rather on the simple side, since it is an easier matter to fill out than to thin down; but it should I think be there. For one's own group, it is perfectly possible to write out (in whole or part) a satisfactory realization which will sound more spontaneous than in fact it is; but a good improvising accompanist is still more satisfactory, and if you have one you may be thankful to spare yourself the trouble – and you will enjoy his contribution all the more because it will be coming out a little differently every time.

In the same way, a few editors have already decided to include sample workings (and I am sure that this is desirable and will increase) for free ornamentation wherever such ornamentation is not merely optional but necessary, as in certain kinds of slow movement which were written down only as a framework, and again as (with moderation) in the repeat of the first section of a da capo aria. Main cadential trills, and appoggiaturas in recitative, are further additions necessary to complete the notes, and are therefore very

often to be indicated in performing editions so that the less experienced performers shall not leave them out.

Accidentals are a further element affecting the notes and requiring
editorial decisions. They were both introduced and notated on
principles which gradually changed, and which are not the same
today as they were in the baroque period. In order for the performer
to be able to draw his own conclusions, a scholarly edition must
show how the notated accidentals stand in the original, which
cannot be done if they are modernized even with due notice given.
For a performing edition (including one's own preparations for
performance), a choice must at some stage be made, which can then
be indicated in the normal modern way.

Conventional alterations by the performer of the notated
rhythms were optional in some contexts, and almost obligatory in
others; they may be suggested in writing or left to rehearsal, but in
any case should be provisionally considered ahead of time.

Marking up the material

The best method will usually be to plot the broad outlines of an
interpretation in advance. The main louds and softs; the chief rallentandos; some phrasings or bowings, and some ideas for articulation
and for tempo: such essential elements must not be left liable to
hesitation, and should therefore be marked in the score and parts
even for experienced performers. But the finer points cannot be
premeditated, succeeding as they do essentially by spontaneous
impulse. These include the small dynamic inflections through recur-
rent troughs and peaks; the tiny pauses and silences of articulation;
the slight stretchings and delayings, placings and timings, and yield-
ings to the varying intensity of the harmony – in fact, everything
that brings life to a performance but cannot be marked in detail
without risking exaggeration or self-consciousness. It is a vital flow;
yet it flows most naturally when the broad plan is already settled.

Preparing a good working text in these and other ways depends
on plenty of rehearsing experience; and good rehearsing depends on
a well-prepared text. For the performer to take his own preparations
in hand so far as he can is both proper and enjoyable, in keeping with
the gloriously permissive spirit of baroque musicianship.

Chapter Three · Shaping the Tempo

Good tempo a variable

Of the many decisions to be taken by the performer, the first to arise and usually the most important is tempo. It is also in some ways the hardest. Notation cannot provide a simple answer, and for baroque music nothing very conclusive is to be found in the written instructions. Composers and editors of later periods have, it is true, sometimes indicated precise tempos by metronome markings. The fatal obstacle remains that good tempo itself is not a precise quality.

In the first place tempo is affected by acoustics. A resonant acoustic causes so much overlapping sound that a good performer will probably feel the need to slow down the fast tempos a little to retain clarity. A dry acoustic, on the other hand, is an invitation to press on with the tempo in the attempt to overcome the lack of responsiveness.

The close connection obtaining between tempo and mood provides a more subjective but no less valid reason for the variability of good tempo. Time-words like allegro (cheerful), adagio (at ease) or grave (serious) specify a mood in order to suggest a tempo. Every performer, however, brings a temperament of his own to his creative partnership with the composer; and nearly all music can be eased a little to the fast side or to the slow side, bringing out rather more of the brilliant or rather more of the expressive potentialities latent within its implications. It is not a matter, therefore, of finding the one right tempo, but of finding a right tempo for one interpretation.

Time-signatures

The baroque period inherited, modified and passed down to us a system of remarkable complexity – and still more remarkable confusion – for measuring the relative durations of notes in proportion to one another. Its earlier forms are called mensural or proportional notation. According to the time-signature, either three or two faster notes might go to each slower note, always provided that the arrangement of notes in different orders, or the presence of dots of various significations, or other rules themselves variable, might intermittently affect this relationship. In medieval and renaissance music it takes a very expert editor to work out a satisfactory performing text in this and other respects, and the margin of uncertainty may remain considerable. In the early baroque period difficulties of mensuration still occur, all the harder because the inconsistencies of the system and its unsuitability to the newer styles of composition were already undermining such credibility as it had ever possessed.

The following Table I may serve as a very much simplified guide to what we might expect to find around the borders of the renaissance and baroque eras.

TABLE I: Signs of mensuration *c.* 1600

SIGN	TIME	PROLATION
☉	Perfect: |o| = o o o	Perfect: o = ♩♩♩
O	Perfect: |o| = o o o	Imperfect: o = ♩♩
ᑕ	Imperfect:|o| = o o	Perfect: o = ♩♩♩
(	Imperfect:|o| = o o	Imperfect: o = ♩♩

DIMINUTION AND AUGMENTATION

⊕	Note values become half those of	O
₵ or Ɔ	„ „ „ „	C
₵ or ⅅ	„ „ „ „	₵
$\frac{2}{1}$	Dupla (diminution): ♩ = previous o	
$\frac{1}{2}$	Dupla (augmentation): o = previous ♩	
$\frac{3}{1}$ or ⅗	Tripla (diminution): o o o = previous o	
$\frac{3}{2}$ or 3	Sesquialtera (diminution): ♩♩♩ = previous o	

The information imparted by these signs concerns relative proportions: how long to hold a note of each nominal value in proportion to those of other nominal values. The mensural system did not itself purport to regulate absolute tempos. There was, however, a further convention associated with it which did purport at least to reflect tempo in the absolute, not directly or strictly, but indirectly and approximately. This was the assumption that the performer always kept time to an actual or imagined beat of the hand, the approximate speed of which everybody was supposed to know. The Latin name for this broadly steady beat was *tactus*; one English name for it was 'stroke'.

(23) Thomas Morley, London, 1597: The stroke [*tactus*] 'is a successive motion of the hand, directing the quantitie of every note and rest in the song, with equall measure, according to the varietie of

signes and proportions'. It allows 'a certayne space or length, wherein a note may be held in singing'.

The stroke of the hand, the *tactus*, was to be at a comfortable speed, and never much faster or slower, so that the tempo, while not by any means rigidly controlled, nevertheless remained constant for each of the numerous proportions under which it might be regulated. This supposition, like the mensural system itself, lost credibility in the baroque era. Baroque tempos in the absolute never can be ascertained merely from 'the varietie of signes and proportions'. Relative tempos can sometimes be ascertained, particularly when there is a change of time-signature in course of a piece, or when different parts show different time-signatures in the same passage. But this too is neither easy nor reliable, because of the confusion inherited and deepened during the long transition.

Thus, for example, it was academic theory and popular supposition throughout the baroque period (and subsequently) that ₵ or Ɔ somehow halves the value or duration of all notes in proportion to the value they would otherwise have had if the signature were C. But already in 1558 Zarlino *(24)* was attacking the entire mensural system with its graphic and numerical signs. In 1597 Morley *(25)* warned that composers were not observing the rule as he had just given it. In 1610 Maillart *(26)* dismissed the 'signs of imperfection' (duple time) as 'superfluous and useless'. By 1650 Kircher*(27)* summed up his own particularly learned and extensive treatment of the subject by calling it 'this most confused material' and 'this utter muddle *(haec tota farrago)*'. Of crossed ₵ in relationship to uncrossed C he tells us that in theory 'the notes must be halved' so as to go 'twice as fast', but that in practice such relationships are shown quite simply 'by the rapidity of our notes, such as minims, crochets, quavers, semiquavers; hence we too judge it superfluous to use those signs; indeed I have found that a majority of the most excellent musicians and the most expert in theory of the present time have deliberately omitted them, and taken them for one and the same sign *(pro unico signo)*'.

But the legend lingered. It was respectable to include the old rule in popular text-books, without Kircher's learning or his practical circumspection. Thus Playford *(28)* in editions of his successful *Introduction* from 1672 asks for Ɔ 'to be Play'd or sung as swift again as the usual measure'. But from 1694, as '*Corrected and Amended by* Mr. Henry Purcell', we find (much more realistically) C as 'the slowest', with four beats two of which go to each tick (probably one second) of a 'large Chamber-Clock'; ₵ 'a little faster'; and Ɔ 'quickest of all'. The relationship here is left indefinite, which is nearer to the facts and not unhelpful so far as it goes.

In his concise text-book *The Principles of Practical Musick*, which had many editions from 1665 onwards, Christopher Simpson *(29)* made the same indefinite distinction, which was common by then, and added as a rough guide for beginners: 'I would have you pronounce these words (*One, Two, Three, Four*) in an equal length, as you would (leisurely) read them', to give four crotchets to the semibreve. Georg Muffat *(30)* in 1695 wrote that 2 or ¢, 'being given in two beats, it is clear that in general it goes as fast again, as this C which goes in four'; but he then gives so many particular departures from this rule that it virtually disappears. Masson *(31)* in 1697 remarked that the only real difference is between duple and triple measures, and in the actual 'quickness' or 'slowness' with which they are taken; Loulié *(32)* in 1696 admitted that 'the practice' of 'these time-signatures' is 'not very certain, some use them in one way, some in another'; Heinichen *(33)* in 1728 put it that 'the signs 2, ₂, C or ¢ are used without discrimination, sometimes for a naturally rapid piece and sometimes for a slow one'.

Even for the *alla breve*, which is always a steady pulse of two (not four) to the semibreve, Heinichen *(34)* remarked somewhat resignedly that this perfectly distinct kind of measure – so significant, for example, in many of the finest fugal movements of J. S. Bach – can quite indiscriminately be 'marked either by C or ¢'. Quantz *(35)* in 1752 described C as the proper sign for 'allabreve or alla capella', but lamented that 'with regard to the aforesaid measure many have fallen into error through ignorance'. Indeed, different manuscripts or early prints of the same piece may show C and ¢ with no possible difference of meaning. As so often, we must take the meaning from the music and not from any such casual inconsistencies in the notation, habitual as these unfortunately are in baroque circumstances.

The situation was no clearer with regard to numerical time-signatures. Thus, for example, 3 or ₃⁄₁ (i.e. ³⁄₁) meant, in proportional notation, take three units in the (previous or assumed) time of one: the ratio is thus 3:1; one name for it was Tripla. Similarly ³⁄₂ meant take three units in the time of two: the ratio is 3:2; one name for this was Sesquialtera. But in course of the long transition through the baroque period these meanings gradually and insensibly declined until, by 1756, Leopold Mozart *(36)* expressed our modern usage in the matter with never a hint that it had ever been any different: 'The top number is the numerator while the bottom number is the denominator. We may therefore say that of those notes of which four go to a bar of common time, two go to a bar of ²⁄₄ time'; and 'in this manner all time measures are calculated'.

In short, the information imparted has ceased to be how long to hold a note in proportion to others. The information is how many notes of what nominal value constitute a bar. Thus we find, for example, that editions of Playford's popular *Introduction* earlier than 1697 explain time-signatures as proportions; but from 1697 onwards, as fractions of the semibreve, in recognition of this newer method, which had evidently taken popular hold by then, though it may have been in growing use for about a quarter of a century before.

In all this conflicting evidence about time-signatures, however, there is one principle of great practical importance which comes up repeatedly. This is that triple-time measures, in whatever manner they may be notated, tend to look much slower than they are meant to sound. Simpson *(37)* in 1665 put it that 'sometimes the *Tripla* consists of *three Semibreves* to a Measure, each *Semibreve* being shorter than a *Minim* in Common Time'; while 'the more *Common Tripla* is *three Minims* to a *Measure*, each *Minim* about the length of a *Crochet* in *Common Time*'. Using the rather different terminology of the eighteenth century, Alexander Malcolm *(38)* warned us in 1721 that 'Movements of the same Name, as *adagio* or *allegro*, etc., are swifter in triple than in common time'; moreover, 'the *allegro* of one Species of *triple* is a quicker Movement than that of another, so very uncertain these things are'. Grassineau *(39)* in 1740 likewise confirmed that 'movements of the same name as Adagio, or Allegro, are swifter in triple than in common Time'. We have here an instruction of very general baroque significance: triple time goes faster than it looks.

Time-words

Once again, confusion was and remains inherent in the baroque use of descriptive words to indicate on the one hand mood, and on the other hand tempo. Our only practical approach is to compare the baroque descriptions, noticing their discrepancies with one another as well as with our own modern conventions.

Purcell *(40)* in 1683 described Largo as 'a middle movement', faster than Adagio and Grave which he gave for 'a very slow movement'. Brossard *(41)* in 1703, however, has: Largo 'VERY SLOW'; Adagio 'COMFORTABLY *at your ease, without pressing on*, thus almost always *slow* and dragging the speed a little '; Lento 'SLOWLY, *heavily*, not at all *lively* or *animated*'; Andante '*to stroll with even steps*'; Allegretto 'RATHER GAILY, but with a gracious, pretty, blithe gaiety'; Allegro 'always GAY, and *decidedly lively*; very often quick and light; but also at times with a *moderate* speed, yet *gay*, and *lively*'; Presto 'FAST . . . the speed must be pressed on, by making the beats very short'; Prestissimo 'very quick'; Assai, either 'much', or 'a judicious *mean* of slowness, and of rapidity' (a useful warning of one possible source of ambiguity).

Malcolm *(42)* in 1721 has: '*Grave, adagio, largo, vivace, allegro, presto*, and sometimes *prestissimo*. The first expresses the slowest Movement, and the rest gradually quicker; but indeed they leave it altogether to Practice to determine the precise Quantity'; for even when '*slow, brisk, swift, etc.*' are written, 'these are still uncertain Measures, since there are different Degrees of *slow* and *swift*; and indeed the true Determination of them must be learnt by Experience from the Practise of Musicians'. For Grassineau *(43)* in 1740 Adagio is 'slowest of any except grave' (which the famous Dr Burney corrected by hand in his copy, now in the British Museum, to 'the slowest of any'); Largo 'one degree quicker than grave, and two than adagio'; Lente or Lento 'much the same as largo'; Allegro 'brisk, lively and pleasant' yet 'without precipitation'; Presto '*fast or quick, gaily yet not with rapidity*'; Prestissimo 'extreamly quicke, hastily, with fury'. C. P. E. Bach and Johann Friedrich Agricola *(44)* in their obituary notice of J. S. Bach shortly after 1750 called him 'very accurate in his conducting and very sure of his tempo, which he usually made very lively', but of course we do not know how lively this may have implied.

(45) Joachim Quantz, Berlin, 1752: Take the tempo 'more from the content of the piece than from the [time-] word'; but 'whatever speed an allegro demands, it ought never to depart from a controlled and reasonable movement'. [Excellent advice, to be taken very seriously into account.]

(46) C. P. E. Bach, Berlin, 1753: 'The tempo of a piece, which is usually indicated by a variety of familiar Italian terms, is derived from its general mood together with the fastest notes and passages which it includes. Proper attention to these considerations will prevent an allegro from being hurried and an adagio from being dragged.' [Excellent advice again.]

Leopold Mozart *(47)* in 1756 included the following terms in ascending order of speed: Grave; Largo; Adagio; Andante; Vivace; Allegretto; Allegro ('which indeed shows a gay, but not hurried tempo'); Presto and Allegro assai ('very little different' from each other); Prestissimo and Presto assai ('almost the same'). Once more he insists that tempo cannot be described in words but 'must be inferred from the music itself, and this is what infallibly shows the true quality of a musician. Every melodic piece includes one phrase at least from which the variety of tempo needed by the music can be clearly recognized. This phrase, if other considerations are taken into account, often compels one into its own natural speed. Bear this in mind, but also realize that for this sort of intuition long experience and fine sensibility are required. Who will contradict me if

I regard this as among the highest accomplishments in the art of music?'

Dance-forms

Something may be learnt from the tempos at which it is necessary to dance certain of the dances whose forms became the basis of instrumental movements *(48)*. Indeed, dances of the renaissance, and to some extent subsequently, were on many occasions both played and sung while the dance proceeded. Under most conditions during the baroque period, however, we are more likely to be confronted with instrumental forms which began as dances, but became more and more distantly removed from the ballroom and more and more liable to ornamental elaborations, as a result of which their tempos changed (usually by slowing down). Even the tempos of the dances themselves were liable to change as the steps, the figures and the social functions altered. While it can be of the greatest value to have danced them, and while the entire lilt and rhythm may be far better acquired by this means, considerable caution is nevertheless needed in drawing conclusions about the tempos. It is particularly important to make sure of comparing the right version of the dance, and in its right historical condition *(49)*.

The pavan has a certain swaying motion at moderate speed, never again to be mistaken by those who have taken part in it; nevertheless, highly ornamented pavans not intended for dancing may need a slower tempo in order to fit in all those elaborate variations gracefully.

The galliard follows at the same pulse-rate as the pavan but in triple time. It is more lively in effect but not in speed, since otherwise the dancer cannot make his energetic motions with just the proper poise and elegance, if indeed he can make them at all (at too slow a speed, on the other hand, he cannot keep an even balance).

The volta always seems to need those fairly steady three pulses in a measure which allow the lady to be raised neatly from the ground while gyrating with controlled impetuosity. You will not get her airborne otherwise.

The saraband ranged from very rapid and vigorous (seventeenth-century England) or moderately slow (Italian) to decidedly slow (France and Germany including J. S. Bach).

The minuet had a similar development from 'a very lively dance' (Brossard *(50)* in 1703) to 'rather moderate than quick' (Jean-Jacques Rousseau *(51)* in 1751–65).

The Allemande was 'very *Ayrey*, and *Lively*' for Mace *(52)* in 1676, but 'a serious and dignified movement and should be so performed' for Walther *(53)* in 1732.

The Italian-style Coranto (in simple triple time) was correctly called 'Lively, Brisk and Cheerful' by Mace *(54)* in 1676, and the French-style Courante (in compound triple time, with its highly characteristic cross-rhythms produced as if by hemiola) was with equal correctness described as taken 'gravely' by Masson *(55)* in 1699.

A piece by Louis Couperin *(56)* appears in manuscript as 'Chaconne or Passacaille', confirming that these two dance titles are in essence no different, though sometimes differentiated: Brossard *(57)* from 1701 and Walther *(58)* pirating him in 1732 gave Passacaglio as 'slower' than Chaconne; yet Quantz *(59)* in 1752, on the contrary, wrote that 'a Passacaille is equivalent to a Chaconne, but is played a little faster'.

With so many variables at issue, only the broadest indications can be had from these and other dance titles; it is as always from the music itself, and the mood in which it is being interpreted, that a good tempo will be found.

Measured timings

Our present compact metronome, using a short compound pendulum in place of a long simple pendulum, was not established until 1816. However, various attempts were made in the baroque period to measure and record actual tempos by comparison with some natural or mechanical constant: by clock-beats or watch-beats (Simpson *(60)* in 1665, Purcell for Playford in 1694, at *(28)* above; Alexander Malcolm *(61)* in 1721); or by some species of pendulum (Loulié *(63)* in 1696, L'Affillard *(62)* in 1705, Tans'ur *(64)* in 1746, Choquel *(65)* in 1759 and others); or by much less exact standards, such as the comfortable hand-stroke of the old *tactus*; or a moderate counting (Simpson at *29* above), or the fastest articulate counting; or a steading walking pace, or a quick pace; or the mean pulse-rate in human beings, which, if taken as 75 a minute, for minims, agrees with a very usual watch-tick of 300 a minute for quavers, i.e. MM = 150, a rather fast allegro. Quantz *(66)* also refers to the human pulse, which being in this case taken as an average of 80 in a minute allows of the following (not wholly realistic) calculations. (See Table 11.)

Neal Zaslaw *(67)* made a most thorough and valuable survey of several such baroque attempts, from which he has extracted all the information to be had, without being able to establish to his own satisfaction any constant foundation for baroque tempos as a whole. He points out that Quantz has bourrée, canarie, gigue, gavotte and passacaille faster, but loure and passepied slower, than the rates he has reconstructed from comparable French sources. The tempos given by Quantz to ordinary time-words seem if anything yet more

TABLE II:
MM numbers based on Quantz

I:	Allegro assai (including Allegro molto, Presto, etc.)	♩ = 160
II:	Allegro (including Poco Allegro, Vivace, etc.)	♩ = 120
III:	Allegretto (including Allegro ma non tanto, non troppo, non presto, moderato, etc.)	♩ = 80
IV:	Adagio cantabile (including Cantabile, Arioso, Larghetto, Soave, Dolce, Poco Andante, Affettuoso, Pomposo, Maestoso, Alla Siciliana, Adagio spiritoso, etc.)	♩ = 40
V:	Adagio assai (including Adagio pesante, Lento, Largo assai, Mesto, Grave, etc.)	♩ = 20

The above values are 'in Common time'.
Double the speed 'in Alla breve time'.

Bourrée [¢ or 2]:		♩ = 160
Canarie:		♩. = 160
Chaconne:		♩ = 160
Courante:		♩ = 80
Entrée:		♩ = 80
Furie:		♩ = 160
Gavotte:	about	♩ = 120
Gigue:		♩. = 160
Loure:		♩ = 80
Marche [¢ or 2]:		♩ = 160
Menuet:		♩ = 160
Musette [3–4]:		♩ = 80
[3–8]:		♪ = 80
Passacaille:	about	♩ = 180
Passepied [3–4]:	about	♩ = 180
[3–8]:	about	♪ = 180
Rigaudon [¢ or 2]:		♩ = 160
Rondeau [¢ or 3–4]:	about	♩ = 140
Sarabande:		♩ = 80
Tambourin:	about	♩ = 180

questionable. It is notoriously difficult for a musician to attach any metronome marking which seems right the next time he comes back to it, as Beethoven used to find out to his own incredulous fury, or Brahms when he wrote to Sir George Henschel that 'the metronome is of no value. As far at least as my experience goes, everybody has, sooner or later, withdrawn his own metronome markings'. Or we might put it with Bemetzreider *(68)* in 1771 that 'taste is the true metronome'. And the reason surely is that tempo itself is not a constant. Tempo is a variable.

Flexibility in baroque tempo

There are, of course, obvious symmetries in baroque music, requiring corresponding regularity of tempo. It may be less obvious, but it is equally important, that there are subtleties within the symmetries, requiring sensitive and imaginative irregularities.

Thus Frescobaldi *(69)* in 1615–16 required his Toccatas 'as we see done in modern Madrigals', to be taken 'now slowly, now quickly, and even held in the air, to match the expressive effects, or the sense of the words'; while 'the cadences, although they may be written quickly, are properly to be very much drawn out; and in approaching the end of passages or cadences, one proceeds by drawing out the time more adagio'; and 'when you find [ornamental] passages and expressive effects, it will be desirable to play slowly'; for 'it is left to the fine judgement of the performer to regulate the tempo'. Mace *(70)* in 1676 recommended 'Liberty . . . to *Break Time; sometimes Faster*, and *sometimes Slower*, as we perceive, the *Nature of the Thing Requires*'. Jean Rousseau *(71)* in 1687 also wanted 'liberties'; for 'there are people who imagine that imparting the movement is to follow and keep time; but these are very different matters'. Couperin *(72)* in 1716 reiterated that 'measure defines the number and time-value of the beats; but cadence [i.e. what he has just called 'cadence or movement'] is properly the spirit, the soul that must be added to it'. And Quantz *(73)* in 1752 summed it up for us when he wrote that 'the performance should be easy and flexible' and 'without stiffness and constraint'.

It is occasionally possible to borrow a little time, but pay it back: e.g. by hurrying on after slowing down, or more probably by slowing down after hurrying on, as when C. P. E. Bach *(74)* suggested in 1753 that certain sequences (or freely sequential passages) 'can be effectively performed by accelerating gradually and gently, and retarding immediately afterwards'. But much more often the need is not for borrowed time but for stolen time (the literal translation of *tempo rubato*).

Baroque music is constructed with many cadences. Most are so transitory that we take them in our stride. Some are a little more weighty in the progressions of the harmony and the movement of the bass: they do not warrant a rallentando, but they do require just sufficient recognition to acknowledge them with a momentary easing of the tempo. The listener is not aware of it, but nevertheless feels at ease, and does not get that monotonous sensation (which used to be more familiar at baroque performances than it is at present) of being driven along with the depressing punctuality of a machine. The tempo is not arbitrary, but it is not ruthless either. The tempo is flexible.

Yet other cadences are clearer still and require quite a perceptible rallentando, usually followed by an equally perceptible pause in the phrasing before the music takes up again in tempo. It is not that these expressive stretchings have necessarily to be very much in themselves: they should often be exceedingly slight. But if the bass and the harmonies are saying cadence, the performers should be saying cadence as well.

There will usually be something in the structure to account for any pronounced sense of cadence. For example, a baroque allegro may often set out its opening material (whether this is simple or multiple) in some shapely exposition, and make it evident both melodically and harmonically when this exposition is winding up. Unless the listener is presented here with a perceptible rallentando, there is an effect of hurry even if it is not noticed as such; and moreover, an important and enjoyable element in the structure of the movement is allowed to go for nothing. It is the same when the development-like section, which is likely to occupy the middle portions of the movement, is drawing to a close, in preparation for the return of the primary material in more or less recapitulatory form. This preparation must be heard to be endorsed by another sufficient although not excessive rallentando, or else, again, this significant aspect of the structure will make little or nothing of its intended effect. There will normally be a concluding rallentando too.

When the music has been shaped merely by an easing of the tempo, the pick-up is usually quite smooth and inconspicuous. When there has been a definite rallentando, it is often better to delay the pick-up by a fleeting moment of poise, so that the new matter can be placed with a certain deliberation which will sound (although it is not) more genuinely punctual than if it had arrived with metronomic accuracy. This deliberate 'placing' of a new section, or merely of a new phrase, is again unlikely to be noticed by the listener. It should not be noticed. But it does in fact constitute a brief allowance of stolen time; for neither the moment of poise itself, nor the rallentando (little or much) which led up to it, is ever going to be restored later in the movement. Such stolen time does not need to be restored; it is simply a normal ingredient of that 'easy and flexible' style recommended by Quantz *(75)*.

It was also C. P. E. Bach's *(76)* opinion in 1753 that 'certain deliberate disturbances of the beat are extremely beautiful' and that 'certain notes and rests should be prolonged beyond their written length for reasons of expression'. But he was cautious teacher enough to warn us that 'in general, ritenutos are better suited to slow or comparatively moderate tempos than to very rapid ones'; and in his subsequent edition of 1787 (when the galant idioms, already employed with dignity by J. S. Bach, were incurring some of the

growing hazards of sentimentality), C. P. E. Bach *(77)* thought it
advisable to add that 'in expressive playing, the performer should
avoid numerous and exaggerated ritenutos, which are apt to cause
the tempo to drag'; for 'the attempt should be made to hold the
tempo of a piece just as it was at the start, which is a very difficult
achievement'. Difficult it is, and important; but so also is the needful
flexibility.

Notated rallentandos

Rallentandos were occasionally written as verbal instructions into
the notation of baroque music: for example, by Matthew Locke *(78)*
in 1675, when in his music for *The Tempest* he included the instructions 'soft and slow by degrees' for diminuendo with rallentando,
'lowder by degrees' for crescendo, and 'violent' for a climax. It
was not, indeed, usually thought necessary to indicate anything
musically so obvious. But when 'adagio' or 'grave' appears within a
few bars of the end of a movement, the intention may not always
be an immediate change to slower tempo (meno mosso) so much as a
steep but not immediate slowing down (molto rallentando), i.e. a
more conspicuous and self-conscious retarding of the tempo than the
normal which would be taken for granted in such a situation. The
phrase may sometimes have the aspect of a tiny coda; and if this
seems to be planned as an echo effect, it should be taken *piano*
whether so marked or not (as quite often it is). We may, conversely,
actually wish to end a movement without rallentando (senza rall. or
senza rit.); but that is a special and not a normal effect – for instance
in those brilliant and witty last movements of very brief extent
which end some sonatas in an Italian style.

A normal cadence implies a normal rallentando. A cadence with
'adagio' written in implies a more than normal rallentando. The
word is then being used, in fact, as Frescobaldi already used it at *(69)*
above, when he wrote of approaching cadences 'which are to be very
much drawn out', where 'one proceeds by drawing out the time more
adagio'. Cases are not infrequent in Italian allegros, and may also be
seen in J. S. Bach, as in the G major Prelude for organ (BWV 550, NBA
IV/v, 138); the B minor organ Fugue (BWV 579, NBA IV/vi, 71); and
the C minor organ Fugue (BWV 575, NBA IV/vi, 26), where the whole
last section is marked 'adagio' (in the simple sense of meno mosso) but
the last half-bar of it is again marked 'adagio' (probably in this
extended sense of più rallentando). The word 'lento' is also found
occasionally in the same sense of more rallentando, or a steeper
rallentando, than it might otherwise occur to the performer to make.
Just as a sequence of *p, mf, f, mf, p* may mean not dynamic steps but a
graded rise and fall, so adagio or grave or lento may under such

circumstances mean not tempo steps but a tempo gradation: in short, an allargando.

Flexibility in recitative

Of all musical textures recitative is the least subject to the notated measure. Recitative evolved in and through the rise of opera, and opera arose in and through the evolution of recitative. There was, indeed, a *stile recitativo* shortly before the rise of opera: it is best called, in English, the reciting style, since at first it merely held the potentiality for recitative. Indeed, the *stile recitativo* continued to include lyrical developments in addition to those declamatory developments which opera required, and to which we now confine the name of recitative in ordinary use.

Recitative is not only declamatory; it is of indeterminate length and open in form, not closed as aria is. It is for the singer to exploit every turn of passion and every verbal inflection; it is for the accompaniment to follow unhesitatingly, or even to press on where mere punctuality would hold the singer back. Opera is drama; and recitative, *stile rappresentativo*, the representative style, as it was alternatively called, is drama in music, no matter whether its setting is the theatre, the church, or the chamber cantata. This fact conditions its entire manner of performance.

Recitative was probably achieved by Peri in his *Dafne* (Florence, 1598 Florentine Old Style, i.e. 1597), the earliest opera, of which unfortunately the music is nearly all lost. Caccini, already a pioneer of the reciting style, emulated it immediately; Monteverdi enriched it; mid-seventeenth-century opera popularized it; Bonini *(79)* in 1615 wrote that 'according to the needs of the words' we should 'sing quickly or slowly, now sustaining, now quickening the beat, for thus demands the Florentine style'. Monteverdi *(80)* in 1615 wanted the *genere rappresentativo* (theatrical style) 'sung without beat', and in 1638 described it as 'sung to the time of the heart's feeling, and not to that of the hand'. Doni *(81)* around 1635 put it that 'in the *stile recitativo* the Singer is not in the habit of confining himself to any beat'. Bonachelli *(82)* in 1642 asked us 'in accordance with the feeling' to beat 'now fast, now slow . . . as indeed anyone will easily know immediately who possesses the fine manner of singing' – i.e. bel canto.

Free and declamatory as this early Italian recitative was both in conception and performance, it was also melodious, carrying as it did the chief musical expression of the opera. By the second half of the seventeenth century, however, the recitative began gradually to become less melodious, and the arias more elaborate, until in the later operas of Alessandro Scarlatti, for example, around the start of the eighteenth century (and still more so a little later in Handel or Hasse), the arias carry the chief musical expression and the recitative may often do little more than string the plot and the dialogue along. Already in 1681 Berardi *(83)* wrote that 'the representative style, that is, of the theatre, consists in this alone, that singing one speaks, and speaking one sings'. And Brossard *(84)* in 1703, perhaps with that actual passage in mind, likewise called *recitativo* 'a manner of Singing which holds as much of *Declamation* as of *Song*, as if one *declaimed* in *Singing*, or as if one *sang* in *declaiming*, hence where one has more attention to expressing the *Passion* than to following exactly a timed measure'. Mattheson *(85)* in 1739 confirmed that recitative 'has freedom, in that it governs itself very much according to ordinary speech'; for 'recitative has indeed a beat; but it does not use it; that is, the singer does not need to bind himself by it'. C. P. E. Bach *(86)* in 1762 agreed that recitatives, unless accompanied with a melodic bass and perhaps other strictly moving parts (i.e. 'accompanied' recitative as opposed to 'simple'), 'are declaimed according to their subject-matter, now slow, now fast, without regard to the measure, even though they are written with bars'.

Neither the more melodious early baroque Italian recitative, nor the less melodious late baroque Italian recitative which increasingly evolved away from it during the closing decades of the seventeenth century until it became a quite different species in the eighteenth century, was confined to opera. All this development occurred, together with the equally distinctive development of aria, no less in oratorio and in cantata, both sacred and secular. It is true that for 'church music' Quantz *(87)* in 1752 thought that 'both expression and tempo should be more restrained than in opera, to show respect for the sacredness of the place'; but in the obituary notice on J. S. Bach, already quoted *(88)*, which C. P. E. Bach and J. F. Agricola published in Mizler's *Musikalische Bibliothek* (1739–54), they described him as 'very accurate in his conducting and very sure of his tempos, which he usually made very lively' – presumably in as well as out of church.

During the closing portion of the seventeenth century, Lully evolved yet another distinctive variety of recitative, the French recitative, derived from early Italian recitative, and maintaining something of the declamatory melodiousness which late baroque Italianate recitative was already discarding in favour of the more speech-like variety. The performance of French recitative is just as closely conditioned by the words; but the composer attempted far more often to indicate subtle fluctuations by changes of time-signature (for a recent study by R. P. Wolf see p. 193 below).

Sometimes these notated changes affect the duration of the notes, sometimes only their pulse and groupings. In theory (as usual) 2 or ¢

means twice as fast as C, and half as fast again as 3; but in practice here (still more than elsewhere) the actual interpretation just cannot always work out that way. Choquel *(89)* wrote in 1759 that 'the measure with two beats' goes 'very much more quickly' than the same notes 'in the measure with four beats' except 'for recitatives', where 'its movement is arbitrary and it is the words which decide it'. Already in 1697, Masson *(90)* wrote that 'the Measure of four quick beats is the same thing as that of two slow beats', and that 'in the recitative of a Motet one beats the Measure, but in that of an opera one neglects it, because he who beats the Measure is obliged to follow the voice'. In 1722 Borin *(91)* wrote that 'the different manners of beating the Measure do not in the least alter the tempo'. But, of course, they do alter the pulse; and this seems to be the primary intention of the many changes of time-signature in French recitative. In every case good declamation should be our guide.

The following are examples where ₵ gives a different pulse from 3, but not a different length of crotchet. In Ex. 1 the second 'Oriane', under ₵, is an echo of the first 'Oriane', under 3 – therefore crotchet necessarily equals crotchet across the change of time-signature. In Ex. 2 the second-time ending under 3 is literally the repeat of the first-time ending under ₵ – therefore, still more evidently, crotchet equals crotchet. The pulse changes. The beat remains constant. Other passages remain ambiguous; others may require twice the speed of C or 3 for ₵ or 2, so that minim equals crotchet. Thus in this matter, too, we do not seem able altogether to resolve the confusion prevailing at the time, and must ultimately take responsibility for our own decisions, as did the baroque performers.

Ex. 1. Jean-Baptiste Lully, *Amadis*, Paris, 1684, ed. H. Prunières, Paris, 1939, p. 200: (a) phrase in 3, (b) echoed in ₵ with no change of note-values:

Ex. 2. Jean-Baptiste Lully, *Ballet des Nations*, Paris, 1670, ed. H. Prunières in coll. ed. 'Comédies-Ballets, III', Paris, 1938, p. 133; first-time ending in ₵, second-time ending in 3, with no change of note-values:

Working rules for tempo

As in most other music, the tempos in baroque music, when everything possible has been discovered from the notation and from the contemporary instructions, remain a performer's responsibility. But the following considerations may be of some general assistance.

(i) Time-signatures *at the start* of a movement, when they are the same in all the parts, may give some information about pulse, but little or none about tempo. When they are not the same in all the parts, they may give definite information about the proportions of the note-values in these different parts relative to one another, rather than about their overall tempo in the absolute. Such time-signatures are in general employed so inconsistently that they carry little weight, telling us as a rule nothing about the piece that we cannot as well learn from the barring or even from the phrasing. Instances are extremely frequent in which one manuscript or early print shows one time-signature, while another shows in the same piece another time-signature, obviously without the slightest difference of intention: C and ₵ are, as we have seen, especially liable to be found exchanged in this perfunctory manner.

(ii) On the other hand, time-signatures *in the course* of a movement can hardly be put there without some deliberate purpose, and require much more respectful attention. Something must be intended to change, whether pulse or tempo or both at once. In theory this change should be exact, in the proportion defined: e.g. $\frac{3}{1}$ (Tripla, for three of the following units in the time of one of the preceding units), or $\frac{3}{2}$ (Sesquialtera, for three of the following units in the time of two of the preceding units); and it is always wise to test whether this exact proportion makes sense. The change of time-signature may be saying no more than rather faster or rather slower; or again, it may be saying very much faster or very much slower. The music itself will tell us, if we are aware of the possibilities and keep an open mind.

(iii) For reasons embedded in the actual practice of proportional notation, as partially inherited by the baroque from the renaissance, triple-time metres are likely to go quicker (often much quicker) than they would appear to us to be notated. We may need to move quite swiftly at three minims or even three semibreves to the bar. Moreover, a change from duple to triple may mean an increase (and often a very great increase) of speed. These principles apply especially in the seventeenth century, but may have some relevance into the eighteenth. It is chiefly a matter of not being scared into inactivity by all those breves and semibreves, which may require, on the contrary, some very lively activity indeed. Once this is appreciated, the music will as usual indicate its own proper tempo to an alert performer.

(iv) Any graphic or numerical sign which is either crossed through by an upright stroke or retorted (i.e. turned round to face the other way) is in theory given twice the speed it would otherwise have had; but in practice this theory may either not work at all, or work only in an indeterminate degree. The general suggestion, if any, may only be a rather faster tempo than before, or than you might otherwise suppose.

In mensural signs which appear as numerical fractions, the lower the denominator (bottom figure) is in relation to the numerator (upper figure), the faster in theory is the speed implied; but this implication cannot be regarded as any more reliable in practice than the last. Moreover, it only holds where proportions (definite or indefinite) were still meant. Where the nominal value and number of units to a bar are meant, the opposite applies. Thus $\frac{3}{1}$ will tend to be *faster* than $\frac{3}{2}$ in old-fashioned tripla and sesquialtera, respectively. But $\frac{3}{4}$ will tend to be *slower* than $\frac{3}{8}$, and $\frac{6}{4}$ than $\frac{6}{8}$, in modern simple and compound triple metres respectively. The change from old-fashioned to modern meanings can be documented around the close of the seventeenth century, but the years of uncertainty extend for some considerable period on either side. No wonder Michel de Saint-Lambert *(92)* in 1707 wrote that the time-signatures 'only indicate the movement of the Pieces imperfectly', so that musicians add time-words 'to supplement thereby the powerlessness of the Sign to express their intention'.

(v) We have seen, however, that time-words were also regarded as ultimately powerless to express the composer's intention. It is of great importance to take baroque time-words in the very free spirit of their own period, not in the rather more exact intention of later periods. For example, Couperin's famous *Les Baricades Mistérieuses* is headed *vivement*, but the mystery is lost, and the poetry too, unless the tempo is kept very moderate. Even in 1768 Jean-Jacques

Rousseau *(93)* could describe passing 'from *grave* to *gai*, or from *tendre* to *vif*, without increasing or decreasing the speed of the beat'.

Handel was particularly easy-going in his use of time-words, not always putting the same word even to alternative versions of the same piece (different manuscripts and early prints of the same version show a similar variability). Handel's opening slow movements are sometimes headed Adagio, sometimes Largo and sometimes Andante, where the intention does not seem to be significantly different. For a modern performer a mental 'con moto' might well be added to a number of Handelian and similar opening movements.

(vi) The most valuable working rule for baroque tempos is not to take the fast movements too fast or the slow movements too slow. Brossard's *(94)* 'moderate' Allegro in 1703; Grassineau's *(95)* Allegro 'without precipitation' and his Presto 'fast . . . yet not with rapidity' in 1740; Quantz *(96)* insisting in 1752 that 'whatever speed an Allegro demands, it ought never to depart from a controlled and reasonable movement'; C. P. E. Bach *(97)* advising us in 1753 to consider 'the fastest notes and passages' so as to 'prevent an Allegro from being hurried and an Adagio from being dragged' – these are the soundest counsels for baroque music generally.

In allegro, steadying the tempo literally leaves time for those subtle nuances of phrasing and placing which make so much more of the music, and which sometimes may actually sound more brilliant to the audience than that tempting turn of speed which aims directly at an effect of brilliance. In adagio, it is extraordinary how all sorts of problems over phrasing, articulation and dynamic inflection fall into place of their own accord so soon as it is decided to move the tempo on a little. It is so necessary in a baroque slow movement to feel you are going somewhere, generally with a certain sense of tension though not of haste; and in a fast movement to retain just that sense of dignity and spaciousness which Couperin *(98)* perhaps meant by being 'more pleased with what moves me than with what astonishes me'. Tempo is indeed the most crucial of all problems of interpretation, in baroque as in most other music, and the surest test of good musicianship.

Chapter Four · Shaping the Line

Sustaining and inflecting

The most important element after tempo in performing baroque music is shaping the line. Melody, and the support of that melody by a bass-line which is itself a melody, and the linear imitation of melody whether by free or by fugal counterpoint: all this goes to the texture of baroque music. Harmony, with its forward impulse, its tensions and its contrasting areas of tonality: that generates the driving force behind the melody and the counterpoint. Rhythm enriches and diversifies the thematic material, and has its own serenity or urgency as the case may be. But in everything which goes to the making of a baroque composition, there is a quality of line. It is by shaping the line in every part and in every dimension that we give meaning to the music.

The first stage in shaping the line is to *sustain* the flow of sound with no increasing, no diminishing and no interruption which is not meaningful. The second stage is to *inflect* the flow of the sound with phrasing, articulation, and dynamic, rhythmic or other modifications which mould it into meaningful patterns. Some of this moulding is intuitive and some of it is deliberate, but all of it depends on the sound first being just reliably there, and not distorted by meaningless fluctuations. That may well be what Couperin (99) had in mind when he wrote in 1716 of the harpsichord that 'it is necessary to sustain a perfect smoothness'; and J. S. Bach (100) also, when he called his Inventions of 1723 'an honest guide . . . to acquire a *cantabile* style of playing'. Not because smoothness is the only requisite; but because it provides the acoustic substance which can then be separated into patterns.

To sustain the line is a technical accomplishment which varies with the instrument, and will not be considered in detail here. To inflect the line also depends upon technical accomplishment, but its general principles will be considered here.

Phrasing and articulation

To inflect the line means to respond to its implicit patterns. One way of making these patterns audible is by phrasing and articulation. Phrasing groups the notes into units of more or less substantial extent. Articulation distinguishes individual notes, or groups them into units of brief extent. Both these are aspects of the same musical resource, which consists in breaking the flow of the sound by separating it into units (ranging from single notes, through pairs of notes or threes or fours or more, to complete phrases), which in turn are compounded into sections and movements.

On whatever the appropriate scale, the separations are necessary to the sense. It is not enough to have them clearly understood in the mind of the performer. They have to be made sufficiently audible to get across to the audience. It is, of course, very possible to over-phrase a baroque performance; but a much more common miscal-culation is to under-phrase it, so that everything may be very musicianly yet rather ineffectual. It is necessary for the audience to experience the patterns; and for this the separations in the line are just as important as the line itself.

This necessity was fully appreciated in the baroque period. Thus Frescobaldi *(101)* in 1615–16 instructed us to pause in the proper places, 'because such a pause prevents confusion between one pas-sage and another'. Mace *(102)* in 1676 refers to 'a kind of *Cessation, or standing still*, sometimes *Longer*, and sometimes *Shorter*, accord-ing to the *Nature*, or *Requiring* . . . of the *Musick*'. Couperin *(103)* in 1716 related phrasing and articulation to fingering, since 'a certain melody, a certain passage, when taken [i.e. fingered] in a certain manner, produces . . . a different effect'. Quantz *(104)* in 1752 advised us 'to avoid, with equal care, separating what belongs together, and joining what comprises more than a single thought and should therefore be separate'; also 'to avoid slurring notes which ought to be detached and detaching notes which ought to be slurred'; also 'to perform the *Cantabile* as a good singer performs it'; while 'it is the quick passages in Allegro which must above all be performed briskly, clearly, with liveliness, with articulation and distinctly'. C. P. E. Bach *(105)* in 1753 agreed that 'in general, the liveliness of allegros is conveyed by detached notes, and the feeling of adagios by sustained, slurred notes . . . even when not so marked'. But it was Marpurg *(106)* in 1755 who gave us the in-valuable information that 'opposed to legato as well as to staccato is the ordinary movement which consists [for keyboard instruments] in lifting the finger from the last key shortly before touching the next note. This ordinary movement, which is always understood [i.e. unless otherwise counter-indicated] is never indicated'.

Our modern understanding of an 'ordinary movement' would be something much nearer to legato than to staccato – as, for example, in the so-called détaché on bowed instruments, which in effect means unseparated sounds produced by separate strokes of the bow. Similarly, we do not on the piano separate the sounds as an ordinary, but only as a particular effect. The baroque conception of an *average* articulation was therefore different from that in which we have been brought up: it is neither joined quite smoothly nor separated very sharply; it is somewhere in the middle between the two extremes. This is a principle which, however liable to exceptions, deserves our most respectful attention whenever the passage is neither cantabile nor energetic, but is indeed average and ordinary. And such passages, when all extremes have been duly recognized, comprise a very high proportion of baroque compositions.

There is an intimate connection between phrasing and articulation on the one hand, and vocal and instrumental techniques on the other hand. In vocal music it is important to establish so far as possible the original underlay of the words, or at least the original principles of underlay. On bowed strings slurs should, except in passages of a certain virtuosity, be kept quite simple, but used with reasonable consistency whether so marked or not. On wind instruments original tonguings and articulation syllables are likewise desirable.

Dynamic contrasts

While some dynamic markings for loud and softs, crescendos and diminuendos, occurred early in the baroque period and became rather more numerous later on, by far the chief reliance was placed, as so often, upon the performer's intelligence and feeling. Caccini *(107)* in the famous preface to his *Nuove Musiche* of 1602 spoke strongly of 'Encreasing and Abating the Voyce' as 'the foundation of Passion'. Domenico Mazzocchi, *(108)* who was unusually scrupulous in notating his intentions, called his dynamic instructions in 1638 'common things, known to everyone' (meaning his intentions rather than his markings, which were certainly not common at the time). Simpson *(109)* in 1659 observed that 'we play Loud or Soft, according to our fancy, or the humour [mood] of the music'. Mace *(110)* in 1676 confirmed this instruction to '*humour* a Lesson [piece] by Playing some *Sentences Loud,* and others again *Soft,* according as they best please your own *Fancy*'.

In 1675, we have seen that Locke's *(111)* music for *The Tempest* included the instructions 'lowder by degrees'; 'violent'; 'soft and slow by degrees'. In 1686 Mylius *(112)* gave us the valuable warning that dynamic markings for successive levels may be indications not for sudden but for gradual changes, where 'one should not fall suddenly from *piano* into *forte* but gradually strengthen the voice, and then let it drop'. Thus *p* followed by *f* followed *ff* quite probably (though not of course necessarily) means crescendo poco a poco, and *ff* followed by *f* followed by *p*, quite probably means diminuendo poco a poco, etc. North *(113)* around 1695 would have us 'learn to fill, and soften a sound, as shades in needlework'. Raguenet *(114)* in 1702 wrote about 'swellings of prodigious length', adding that the Italians 'in their tender airs soften the voice insensibly and at last let it die outright'. Alessandro Scarlatti *(115)*, also in 1702, wrote of 'the *pianos* and *fortes* of the instruments' as 'the light and shade which make any singing and playing agreeable'. Scipione Maffei *(116)* in 1711 commended performers who gave 'particular delight to their listeners' by the effective use of *'piano* and *forte'*. Quantz *(117)* in 1752 advised us that 'light and shade must be continuously introduced' – on the performer's initiative – by 'the incessant inter-change of loud and soft'; but here he was presumably thinking of the latest 'galant' idioms, rather than of the typically baroque idioms, where much steadier though by no means rigid dynamic levels are ordinarily implied.

Quantz *(118)* actually wanted the volume of each individual chord increased or diminished to match its degree of dissonance or consonance, though he granted that 'good judgement and sensitive-ness of soul must also play a part'. C. P. E. Bach *(119)* replied in 1753 that 'it is impossible to describe the contexts suitable to the *forte* or the *piano'*, while agreeing that 'it is broadly true that discords are performed loud and concords soft'. This principle in itself is valid, and of the widest relevance. Thus a preparation, being a concord, will ordinarily be softer than the clash of the ensuing discord itself (whether suspended or freshly struck), and the resolu-tion, being also a concord, will ordinarily be yet softer, thus giving the natural rise and fall of the progression. But we are reaching here the finest nuances, which it is quite certainly undesirable to try to notate into the parts. If they will not come out right by nature, they will not come out right by artifice.

Dynamic structure

The broader dynamic structure, on the other hand, repays some consideration prior to rehearsal, and should as a rule be notated editorially into the score and parts. Not only must it be well worked out; it must be performed with decision. There is no objection to planning it differently for different performances, but in any one performance it needs to be entirely purposeful. Marking up the parts is a sensible precaution and avoids any risk of being vague as a result of momentary hesitation.

Most allegros will start loud from their probable nature, and may well continue so (unless contra-indicated by markings or otherwise) until a more contemplative middle section follows the first implied rallentando of any substance. A soft here is often appropriate, and this too may best continue without fussy alteration until the next important rallentando prepares the return of the opening material, which can then come back firm and loud, possibly continuing so to the end. That at least is a scheme which makes good sense with the musical structure if it is simple.

If the musical structure is more complex, so will be the dynamic structure. The principle throughout is to bring in these decisive changes of loudness not merely in order to make a contrast for its own sake, but in order to bring out a contrast already latent in the music. It is not a question of repressing those lesser inflections of volume (and also of rhythm) which are the very life of a melody on all instruments capable of making them. It is a question of giving a stable basis to the flexible expression; and this is the valid reality behind the somewhat misleading suggestion that baroque dynamics are 'terrace-dynamics' held constant over entire passages. There are indeed very many long passages which make best sense on one basic level; but only on the organ or the harpsichord does it come natural not to inflect that level spontaneously as you go along. And even then, of course, inflexibility is somehow not at all the effect conveyed in a good performance. There are so many other factors making for flexibility.

Echoes and humps

Certain special dynamic effects were also current and may be freely used. One is the echo, sometimes in course of a movement but more often at the end, the last few bars then being taken (and sometimes marked) *piano* as a repeat of what has just been heard *forte*. It is usually quite easy, at the end of a movement, to spot this intention and to carry it out even when it is not marked – less easy to spot, perhaps, but still worth watching for, in course of the movement. The word 'adagio' over the last few bars is sometimes a clue for an echo effect, though probably, as we have seen, meaning not so much *meno mosso* as *poco* (or if necessary *molto*) *allargando*.

Another special effect is the *messa di voce* (literally, the 'placing of the voice'), a term used for starting a note *piano*, increasing gradually to *forte*, and decreasing as gradually to *piano*: in short, a hump. This was a familiar recourse of the virtuoso bel canto singers already in the sixteenth century (since Caccini *(120)* noted it in 1602 and probably learned it from his revered teacher delle Palle); it was widely imitated by solo instrumentalists like the trumpeter Fantini *(121)* in 1638 (beginning long notes '*piano*, and then increasing up to half the length of the note, and with the other half falling'); and it was still in full fashion at the end of the baroque period and beyond. Thus C. P. E. Bach *(122)* wrote in 1762 that 'when the solo part has a long sustained note which by the conventions of good perform- ance should begin *pianissimo*, increase by degrees to a *fortissimo*, and return in the same way to a *pianissimo*, the accompanist must follow with the greatest exactitude'. (Tosi in 1723 – see (20) – had however advised the *messa di voce* only in moderation.)

Thus, for example, the long notes which open up the violin entries in the first movement of J. S. Bach's C major Trio Sonata invite a *piano* start, rising to *mezzo-forte* or *forte* and sinking back to *piano* before the continuation in short notes. (The continuo bass moves steadily in quavers meanwhile, and, contrary to C. P. E. Bach's advice, seems here to need a constant *mezzo-forte*, which the violins subsequently match.) The music implies the nuance; and there are plenty of such instances throughout the baroque period. It was, however, always regarded as a special effect, and not as a habitual recourse. It is not intended for movements in which most of the notes are slow and of which the character is tranquil. Dynamic lozenges in such a passage sound quite unauthentically mannered and inappropriate. The point of the *messa di voce* lies in the contrast between its expressive shaping and the quicker notes adjacent to it.

Quicker notes may also, as an occasional but not as a regular treatment, be given brief dynamic lozenges, described by Geminiani *(123)* in 1751 as a 'Swelling of the Sound' on either long or short notes, but shown in his examples (by a special sign ◡) only on a very small proportion of selected notes. The effect on long notes may amount to a normal *messa di voce* and on short notes to an expressive *sforzando*, likewise intended as a special and not as a habitual effect. Leopold Mozart *(124)* required in 1751, it is true, 'a small though barely audible softness at the start of a stroke; for otherwise no note would result'; and 'this same softness must also be heard at the end of every stroke'. This, therefore, is not intended as an expressive effect at all, but as a technical instruction for getting a pure attack and release. David Boyden in his great work on the baroque violin *(125)* would prefer us to regard it as not audible at all. Leopold Mozart's admired model Tartini *(126)* recommended similarly in 1760 'laying the bow lightly on the strings' before pressing, which can then be done 'immediately' (*subito*: not 'gradually' as Dr Burney *(127)* mistranslated this) without sounding 'coarse or harsh'. These passages have been misunderstood *(128)* as indicating a basic crescendo-diminuendo stroke which David Boyden regards as unauthenticated, but which has been accepted, it is only fair to add, by some excellent Continental authorities, as a result of mistaking, as I think, a special effect for a habitual recourse. Lozenge-dynamics should be the exception, not the rule.

There was, I should prefer to say, no one basic stroke, but a great variety. Thus John Hsu *(129)* has brilliantly demonstrated that in French viol bowing, for example, the accepted starting-point was an attack as sharp, it was said, as the plucked strings of the harpsichord, in contrast with Italian violin bowing 'whose changes' as described by Hubert le Blanc *(130)* in 1740 'are imperceptible' (i.e. in cantabile passages). But John Hsu also showed that the French evolved other strokes, some of which were swelled more or less gently while some were sustained more or less firmly. There is nothing in any of this to surprise a true string player. Like the vibrato, the many nuances of the bow are natural resources which must be used appropriately but not ignored for baroque music. The baroque bow itself helps towards using them appropriately.

Vibrato

The line is coloured rather than shaped by vibrato, but it does affect the expressive outline, and may be considered here. Vibrato requires great discretion in baroque music, but there are good acoustic as well as historical reasons for including it in proper moderation.

Recent acoustical researches put the time-span after which it is possible for our own faculties to perceive a new aural event (and indeed other kinds of event) as such, and not merely as an undifferentiated continuation, at about one-twentieth to one-eighteenth of a second. Any absolutely unvarying persistence of the same aural signal beyond this time-span very rapidly fatigues that band of fibres in the basilar membrane of the ear which is involved in detecting it: there is then a subjective decline both in the volume and and in the colourfulness of the sound perceived. It seems to go a little dead on us; and this is the acoustic consideration which makes vibrato a natural rather than an artificial recourse on melodic instruments. The vibrato just mitigates that deadening persistence.

Vibrato is a more or less slight frequency (pitch) modulation combined with a still slighter element of amplitude (loudness) modulation, which, however, very often assumes an apparent prominence, so that we experience something more like a soft tremolo. Experiment shows that the rate of modulation preferred is around six pulsations per second, and the degree of differentiation variable but by no means excessive. Very fast or narrow vibrato becomes unpleasantly agitated; very slow or wide vibrato becomes heavily obtrusive: the happy mean varies with the context but is certain in any baroque music to be moderate. For vibrato on close chords or counterpoint, the range of pitch must be small enough to produce no uncertainty about the harmony. Romantic contexts tolerate more and classical contexts tolerate less vibrato; but the use

of enough vibrato to enliven without confusing the flow of the
sound has ample historical support. There is also good evidence for a
rather different use of a more prominent vibrato, serving on certain
selected notes as a specific ornament.

Sylvestro Ganassi *(131)* at Venice in 1542 and Martin Agricola
(132) at Wittenberg in 1545 already described the 'trembling' *(zit-
tern)* of the left-hand fingers which on stringed instruments produces vibrato: 'one shapes with the free trembling the sweet sound
of the melody' is Agricola's rather poetical description for it in
connection with the 'Polish violin'. Michel Praetorius *(133)* at
Wolfenbüttel in 1619 recommended for singers a 'fine, pleasing
trembling and shaking voice ... but with moderation'. Marin
Mersenne *(134)* at Paris in 1636 called 'the tone of the violin most
ravishing' when sweetened 'by a certain trembling', adding for the
lute that 'the left hand must swing with great violence'. Christopher
Simpson *(135)* at London in 1659, Thomas Mace *(136)* at London in
1676 (with the instruction: 'wave' the fingers 'upwards, and down-
wards') and Jean Rousseau *(137)* at Paris in 1687 (who wrote of
'varying the finger on the fret' of the viol) were among those who
requested a pronounced vibrato as an ornament for conspicuous use
on certain notes; yet Rousseau also recommended a normal vibrato
'in all contexts where the length of the note permits'; it 'should last
as long as the note'. Francesco Geminiani *(138)* at London in 1751
instructed the violinist 'to move the Wrist in and out slowly and
equally' for an expressive vibrato on long notes, but added that
'when it is made on short Notes, it only contributes to make their
Sound more agreeable and for this Reason it should be made use of
as often as possible'. Leopold Mozart *(139)* at Augsburg in 1756
called vibrato 'an adornment which arises from nature herself', and
which can be imitated 'on the violin' by 'a small movement' of 'the
whole hand'; but 'since it is not purely on one note but sounds
undulating, so it would be a mistake to give every note' the vibrato,
like 'some performers who tremble on every note without exception
as if they had the palsy'.

Vibrato as an ornament in baroque music should be massive
enough to draw attention to itself, but only occurs on certain notes
selected for reasons of expression. Vibrato as tone-colouring should
be light enough not to draw attention to itself, but may occur
freely. It is not authentic to exclude vibrato from baroque music. It
is not appropriate to introduce it continuously. Excepting as an
ornament, baroque vibrato differs from romantic vibrato in being
less intense, less sustained, less insistent in every way, but certainly
not in being altogether absent. How much is used depends to a very
large extent on taste, as it always has; more still on the actual character
of the passage, the final arbiter in all such matters of educated

judgement and experience. But the neutral effect of lacking any vibrato where vibrato should naturally be is somewhat unfeeling, and runs contrary to some excellent historical and artistic precedents.

Dynamic balance

We have also to get a good dynamic balance between the parts of an ensemble. There is, for example, a special art involved in contrapuntal music, where entries of the main theme need bringing out with a certain added significance (not necessarily added volume) over and above the subsidiary material surrounding them.

Zacconi *(140)* put it in 1592 that 'entries should be emphasized a little so as to be instantly and clearly perceived by the listener'. Quantz *(141)* in 1752 still asked us to bring out the principal subject by 'a distinctive manner of performance . . . as well as by loud and soft'; and with regard to trio sonatas in particular, he suggests that normally 'the increase and decrease of tone occurs at the same time' in the two solo parts; but that when one part has merely 'to fill in the harmony, it must be performed more softly than the other which makes the principal melody meanwhile', while 'if the parts imitate one another, or make passages which come together either in thirds or in sixths, the one and the other can play at the same strength'. Again in 1752 Avison *(142)* explained that 'when the inner Parts are intended as Accompanyments only, great Care should be taken to touch them in such a Manner, that they may never predominate, but be always subservient to the principal Performer, who also should observe the same Method, whenever his Part becomes an Accompanyment; which generally happens in well-wrought Fugues and other full Pieces, where the Subject and Air are almost equally distributed'. This can only be done with 'every Performer', he shrewdly adds, 'listening to the other parts, without which he cannot do Justice to his own'.

In baroque music the bass-line is usually so interesting and independent a melody in its own right that it requires to be shaped just as imaginatively as any upper part. L'Abbé Laugier *(143)* in 1754 went so far as to say 'furnish all the parts sufficiently, to see that each makes its effect, that the chief parts, such as the treble and the bass, stand out to advantage', and in particular 'one cannot too strongly recommend furnishing the basses beyond the rest; for they are the foundation of the harmony'.

In chamber music, too, the bass must on no account be kept down below the upper melody. On the contrary, it must give not only firm but elegant support. A baroque bass part should not as a rule be made nearly so marcato as is often done: least of all should it be marcato at the heel of the bow, which gives a very exaggerated and

anachronistic effect. It may well partake of that 'ordinary' movement as described above: neither legato, nor staccato, but just a
fluent pulsing, in which no two successive notes will be sustained or
emphasized exactly alike, but the whole dignified line will be alive
with good phrasing and dynamic nuance.

Above all, however, must the bass provide an absolutely reliable
and responsive support for the harmony. The shaping of the bass-
line is conditional upon the progressions of the harmony, just as,
conversely, the intervals of the bass supply the ground-plan on which
the harmonies unfold. We can never afford a weak bass-line in
baroque music.

Accentuation

Normal accentuation results from a momentary silence of articulation followed by a dynamic emphasis. Organs and harpsichords,
having little control by touch over dynamic level, simulate accentuation successfully by the silence of articulation alone. The effect of
accentuation can be further increased by prolonging the note which
carries or simulates the accent: this is sometimes called 'agogic
accent'. The more subtle resources of accentuation are the most
commonly appropriate in baroque music. One of the most effective
is the silence of articulation followed by a crisp attack rather than a
massive weight, and rendered more effective by that slight prolong-
ation which can draw momentary attention to a note without in the
least forcing it. Articulate accentuation and flexible timing work in
very well together for giving a well-moulded shape to a melodic line.

Most phrases can be felt as going to a certain note, often though
not always the top of the phrase, from which the phrase may then
fall away again. This is commonly matched by a crescendo and
diminuendo, and capped by an accent on the pivotal note. Leopold
Mozart *(144)* put it that 'in lively pieces the accent is generally taken
on the highest note'. We may then treat the previous notes almost
like a sort of protracted up-beat to the climax, wherever it may
arrive, and perhaps place that climax just perceptibly late for added
significance. The audience will not experience it as late, but as
properly spacious and proportionable. Geminiani *(145)* actually
warned us in 1751 that 'if by your manner of bowing you lay a
particular Stress on the Note at the Beginning of every Bar, so as to
render it predominant over the rest, you alter and spoil the true Air
of the Piece'. In accentuation, as in so many other aspects of baroque
performance, the subtle flexibility beneath the obvious symmetry is
what averts monotony and brings out significance even from the
most regular-seeming succession of notes. On paper there is nothing
to choose between one note and the next: they all look alike. In

performance, the art is to make them just different enough for the sense to emerge.

Syncopation and hemiola

Syncopations at rapid and moderate speed make their effect swiftly enough to displace the operative accent from its normal place, so that the beat is momentarily challenged. This effect can be greatly enhanced by shortening the note before the syncopated note (i.e. by a minute silence of articulation but in this case without any delay in the timing); and by then accenting the note of syncopation, allowing its ensuing resolution to die away. Leopold Mozart *(146)* puts it for the violin in 1756 that 'you must not forget to attack the middle note [i.e. the syncopated note] more strongly with the up-bow stroke, and to slur the third note [i.e. the note of resolution] to it with a gradual diminution of the volume'. He confirms this in his illustration by setting a staccato dash over the note before the syncopated note. On the organ or the harpsichord, the mere shortening of the note before the syncopated note, if decisively enough executed, will simulate the required accent on the syncopated note. This, however, is merely a particular application of the general principle: precede an accent, if you can make one, and simulate it, if you cannot, by a silence of articulation before it which will do at least half the work, and where necessary, all the work. This is one of the key secrets of baroque articulation.

A rather different manner of displacing the accent is by that cunning effect of cross-rhythm known as the hemiola or hemiolia (literally, one-and-a-half, i.e. in the proportion of 2:1). This occurs in triple time when, for example, two measures of $\frac{3}{4}$ are in effect combined to make one measure of $\frac{3}{2}$. Instead of '*one* two three, *one* two three', we hear '*one* two, *three* one, *two* three'. Thus the accent normally due on 'one' of the second $\frac{3}{4}$ measure is suppressed and should not be sounded; but the 'one' and the 'three' of the first $\frac{3}{4}$ measure, and the 'two' of the second $\frac{3}{4}$ measure, should be strongly sounded. For a conductor, a simple manner of indicating the change of accent is as follows (beat = beat):

TABLE III: Suggestion for beating hemiola

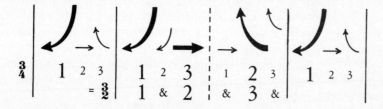

The hemiola normally occurs at the approach to a cadence, whether final, or merely passing. It can often be recognized by 'three' of the first $\frac{3}{4}$ measure being tied to 'one' of the second $\frac{3}{4}$ measure in the bass, but this does not always occur. Sometimes the change is actually notated as a $\frac{3}{2}$ bar in a $\frac{3}{4}$ passage – in which case there is, of course, no difficulty in recognizing the intention. Occasionally, even in the baroque period, the change is notated by a rare survival of proportional time-signatures correctly if somewhat belatedly used in combination with a variety of coloration known as black notation *(147)*. Where no such hint or indication is given by the notation, the change has to be recognized by ear, partly from the contour of the melody, partly from the movement of the harmony. This comes quite easily with a little practice, but it is most important to get it right, since the passages in which a hemiola is undoubtedly intended though in no manner notated are extremely numerous in Corelli, Purcell, Vivaldi, Handel, Bach and others. The effect of thus momentarily displacing the accent one level up in the rhythmic hierarchy is remarkably subtle and enjoyable.

The following Ex. 3 shows a typical hemiola in Carissimi, (a) as normally notated with no indication beyond the implied hint of the tie in the bass across the (inoperative) bar-line, (b) as explicitly but exceptionally notated in full at a matching passage above the same bass, later in the composition; thus confirming that in (a) the accentuation indicated in editorial square brackets is indeed correct.

Ex. 3. Giacomo Carissimi, cantata 'Amor mio', Bologna, Lib. of Conserv., MS V289, (a) mm. 29–32; (b) mm. 69–71 with identical bass, differently notated.

In Ex. 4 an equally typical hemiola in Handel does not tie the bass across the bar-line, but the contour of the upper melodies and the harmonic progression alike require the hemiola rhythm so soon as they are considered in that light; and thus it is in countless passages of the kind. Like so much else in good baroque performance, the beauty of the correct accentuation is simply that it does sound so natural to the music.

Ex. 4. George Frideric Handel, Trio Sonata Op. 11 No. 8, last movement mm. 18–20, hemiola not notated but needed as shown by me in square brackets:

Chapter Five · Shaping the Rhythm

Rhythmic alteration

There were certain complications in the notation and performance of rhythm during the baroque period which affect the shaping of the line. Rhythms written in one way by the composer may allow or even require rendering in another way by the performer. The rules and habits governing such rhythmic alteration were never clear or consistent even for one place and time, still less over the baroque period as a whole. Nevertheless, they were not merely arbitrary options.

Inequality

Throughout and even before the baroque period, and through all national traditions, evidence is found for an expressive practice now commonly described as inequality: the unequal performance of notes notated equally.

(148) Loys Bourgeois, Geneva, 1550: Perform crotchets 'two by two, remaining longer on the first, than on the second'.

(149) Fray Tomás de Santa María, Valladolid, 1565: For crotchets the method is 'to linger on the first, to hurry on the fourth', yet 'not too hurried, but only slightly so'; and with quavers either 'linger on the first quaver and hurry on the second', or 'hurry on the first quaver, linger on the second', etc.

(150) Girolamo Frescobaldi, Rome, 1615/16: Perform the second of each pair of semiquavers 'somewhat dotted'. [Notice that 'dotting' means unequalizing 'somewhat', i.e. not exactly but variably.]

(151) Giovanni Domenico Puliaschi, Rome, 1618: Perform equally notated pairs 'now by dotting the first note, now the second, as the passage requires'.

(152) Anonymous English about 1660: Unequalize 'by stealing half a note from one note and bestowing it upon the next note'.

(153) Bénigne de Bacilly, Paris, 1668: 'Of two notes one is commonly dotted' but 'it has been thought proper not to mark them for fear of getting used to performing them by jerks'; for they must in most cases be 'dotted with such restraint that it is not obvious'; and indeed 'in some passages it is even necessary to avoid dotting altogether'. [Again notice the variable degree of inequality meant by 'dotting'.]

(154) Roger North, English, about 1690: 'In short notes' inequality 'gives a life and a spirit to the strokes, and a good hand will often for that end use it, tho' not express't' [in notation].

(155) Alessandro Scarlatti, Naples, 1694: 'one plays in equal time' the equally notated quavers in a passage which would otherwise be thought to invite inequality.

(156) Georg Muffat, Augsburg, 1693: In a slow two-time 'several quavers continued in succession' should not be unequalized 'for elegance of performance', as they would ordinarily be 'in common time'.

(157) Étienne Loulié, Paris, 1696: 'In each measure but especially triple measure, the half-beats are performed in two different ways, although they are notated in the same way. 1. They are sometimes made equally' as 'in melodies of which the sounds move by leap'. [The Amsterdam edition of 1698 added, but mistakenly, as can be seen from quotations just given above: 'and in all kinds of foreign music where you never dot them except where marked'.] And '2. Sometimes the first half-beats are made a little long' as 'in melodies of which the sounds move stepwise'. Alternatively, 'the first half-beat is made much longer than the second, but the first half-beat ought' in that case to be notated 'with a dot'.

(158) Sébastien de Brossard, Paris, 1701/3, s.v. Andante [i.e. the Italian variety with striding quaver basses] 'means above all for Basso-Continuos, that all the notes must be made equal, and the sounds well separated'. [This is true also for many similar bass parts in Allegro.]

(159) Michel de Saint-Lambert, Paris, 1702: Certain notes are made unequal 'because the inequality gives them more grace [but no rule is final, because] taste judges of this as it does of tempo'.

(160) Jacques M. Hotteterre, Paris, 1707: 'Quavers are not always to be played equally', since 'in some measures there should be a long one and a short one' – especially in 'two in a bar, $\frac{3}{4}$ and $\frac{6}{4}$'.

(161) Michel de Montéclair, Paris, 1709: Notes tend to be 'equal in C, $\frac{2}{4}$ and $\frac{3}{8}$' but 'unequal in ordinary triple 3'. However, it is very hard to

give general principles as to the equality or inequality of notes, 'because it is the style of the pieces to be sung which decides it'; but broadly 'the notes of which four go to a beat are intended to be unequal, the first a little longer than the second'; or two to a beat in triple-time slow movements.

(162) François Couperin, Paris, 1716/17: 'We write otherwise than we perform', whereas [but our other evidence again shows this to be an over-statement] 'the Italians on the contrary write their music in the true values which they have conceived for it. For example, we dot [in performance] several quavers [which follow] in succession by step: and yet we notate them equal.'

(163) Pier Francesco Tosi, Bologna, 1723: 'When over the equal movement of a Bass, which proceeds slowly from quaver to quaver, a Singer' goes 'almost always by step with inequality of motion.'

(164) Michel de Montéclair, Paris, about 1730: In simple 2, 'the first quaver lasts almost as long as if it were followed by a dot, and the second [goes] almost as quickly as a semiquaver'. In $\frac{3}{2}$, 3, $\frac{3}{4}$ or $\frac{6}{4}$ 'the quavers are unequal'. In $\frac{2}{4}$ or $\frac{3}{8}$ 'the quavers are equal. The semiquavers are unequal.' [But definite instructions such as these, though frequent, are not consistent in different French authors.]

(165) Michel Corrette, Paris and Lyons, about 1740: 'The four-time C or ₵ is much used in Italian music', in which 'it is necessary to dot the semiquavers two by two.' Of French 2 time, 'the Italians never use it. The quavers must be made unequal two by two, that is to say make the first long and the second short.' [It may be said that] 'the $\frac{2}{4}$ or $\frac{2}{8}$ is the 2-time of the Italians', in which 'the quavers must be performed equal, and the semiquavers made unequal'; while 'the $\frac{12}{8}$ is found in Italian, German, French and English music', where 'the quavers must be performed equal and the semiquavers made unequal'.

(166) Michel Corrette, Paris, 1741: 'The quavers are performed equally in [some kinds of] Italian music such as may be instanced in the Courante of Corelli's Sonata Op. v No. 7' [a movement notable for leaps rather than steps – see Ex. 14a below]. 'But in French music the second quaver in each beat is performed more quickly.'

(167) Joachim Quantz, Berlin, 1752 (also in French, with slight verbal differences partly used here):
[a] 'It is necessary in pieces of a moderate speed and even in adagio for the quickest notes to be played with a certain inequality, even though they appear at sight to be of the same value; so that at each figure the accented notes, namely the first, third, fifth and seventh

[etc.], must be leant upon more than those which pass, namely the second, fourth, sixth and eighth [etc.], though they must not be sustained so long as if they were dotted.'

[*b*] 'This no longer happens, however, so soon as these notes are found mixed in with figures of notes yet quicker or half as short in the same time; for then these latter' are the ones to be played with 'the first and the fourth notes a little leant upon, and their tone made a little louder than that of the second and fourth notes'.

[*c*] But inequality is precluded on notes 'in a very quick movement, where the time does not permit of playing them unequally, and where we can therefore only apply length and strength on the first of the four'; also on unslurred staccato notes; also on notes bearing dashes or dots of articulation; also on 'several notes on the same pitch'; also 'when there is a slur over more notes than two'; also with 'quavers in gigues'. For 'all these notes ought to be taken equally, the one no longer than the other'.

[*d*] 'If in a slow allabreve or in ordinary common time there is a semiquaver rest on the accented beat, followed by dotted notes, you must take the rest as if it had a dot attached to it, or [another] rest of half its value, and as if the note after it [though written as a semiquaver] were a demisemiquaver' [i.e. inequality applies to rests as well as to notes].

There is no reliable system of inequality to be pieced together from this or any other available evidence. But the following suggestions, supported by the evidence above, may help to keep our use of inequality within the appropriate boundaries of style.

(i) *No inequality at all is admissible:*

If verbal counter-indications appear (*tempo eguale, note eguale, egualmente, notes égales, coups égaux*, etc.).

If staccato signs (dashes, wedges, dots, etc.) appear above or below the notes, or verbal instructions appear to that effect – *staccato, marcato, détachez, notes martelées, mouvement décidé* or *marqué*, etc. – or if, with no particular indication in the notation, the passage is being taken staccato.

If the notes otherwise eligible are too fast to be acceptable without undue jerkiness as unequal figures, or too slow to be accepted as falling into distinctive figures at all.

If notes which might otherwise be eligible are slurred or grouped in any combination excepting in pairs, or if the sense of the music itself prevents them from falling naturally into pairs.

(ii) *Inequality is likely to be undesirable:*

If the character of the music is neither lilting on the one hand, nor vigorous on the other hand, but of a somewhat restrained and

four-square disposition (some baroque authors put the allemande
into this category).

If the intervals of the melody go mainly by leap (as in the
Courante of Corelli's Op. v No. 7, described by Corrette *166*
above as not eligible for inequality); or if it has the kind of steady
purposefulness, largely by leap, which is common in the bass-line of
andantes and certain types of allegro movement, especially of an
Italian character (as prescribed to be taken equally by Brossard at
158 above).

If the speed of notes otherwise eligible, while not unacceptably
fast or slow, is nevertheless not altogether comfortable for the
purpose (there being a fair margin here for individual judgement).

(iii) *Some degree of inequality is likely to be desirable:*
    If the character of the music is either lilting (in which case the
inequality may be slight, often approximating to a triplet rhythm),
or vigorous (in which case the inequality may be pronounced, often
approximating to a dotted or even – rather exceptionally – to an
overdotted rhythm).

If the intervals are slurred in pairs or are naturally grouped in pairs.

If the intervals go paired mainly by step (either liltingly as in the
later and smoother varieties of saraband, in the chaconne and passacaille, and in many others of the more graceful dance forms, on the
one hand; or vigorously as in some of the more energetic, such as the
bourrée, the rigaudon or the gavotte on the other hand). Leaps
between one pair and another do not discourage inequality, since
this can only happen *within* the pairs. Moreover, a *few* leaps within
the pairs can acceptably be included in the inequality; but not too
many.

When inequality appears to be acceptable and desirable, the notes
which are eligible for inequality are those which are the fastest to
occur in substantial numbers within the passage. A *small* number of
faster notes can be ignored for the purposes of this test, in which case
they may either be left equal, or (if not too fast) be made unequal
too. A *large* number of faster notes (if too fast to be themselves
eligible instead of the next slower notes) preclude inequality. And
on the other hand, if the fastest notes to appear in substantial
numbers within the passage go slower than two to a beat, inequality
is probably precluded. Thus, in effect, notes which, other conditions being favourable, are eligible for inequality, will neither be
very fast nor very slow.

(iv) *Inequality may be not only desirable but necessary:*
    If verbal indications appear – *note diseguale, note puntate, note
lunghette, inégales, notes inégales, pointer* (literally 'dot'), *lourer*
(literally 'tie'), *couler* (literally 'slur'), etc.

If inequality is indicated in a corresponding passage, or in one or more parts though not in all parts, or at the beginning but not afterwards, or in some other way best carried through consistently.

There can be two directions for inequality:

Straightforward inequality lengthens the first note of a pair and shortens the second note. In lilting rhythm approximating to triplets, a slur may be added if not already notated; and there is then a sighing fall, each pair being a little separated from the next. It is quite possible to notate this effect by re-barring $\frac{3}{4}$ in $\frac{9}{8}$, or by written triplets (see *168* below). In vigorous rhythm approximating to dotted notes, a slur need not be added: on the contrary, it is often good to treat the lengthening as a silence of articulation, by inserting mentally not a dot but a dot's worth of rest; and so far from making a sighing fall, to stab (*stoccare*) at the figure energetically. It is again quite possible to notate this effect into the score and parts with dotted notes, or with rests instead of dots. But it should be made clear that, whether improvised or preconcerted or written into the prepared text, none of these rhythms implies a mathematical exactness, but on the contrary a natural flexibility.

Reversed inequality lengthens the second note of a pair after shortening the first. This can be done in lilting passages, with an approximation to triplet rhythm (a slur probably being added if not already notated) which in fairly slow time will give a still more sighing fall. Reversed inequality can also occur in vigorous rhythm at fairly fast speed, with an approximation to dotted rhythm in reverse. This can be either slurred or detached, but in either case the accent occurs on the first note of the pair and each pair is still separated a little from the next.

In deciding how far, if at all, to notate into the prepared text an approximation to some inequality which is wanted in performance, it is perhaps worth remembering that marking up the parts has, in general, considerable advantages, even for groups who know very well what they are about. A timely marking may prevent just that momentary hesitation under conditions of stress which can happen to the best performers.

(*168*) *C. P. E. Bach, 1753:* 'Now that triplets have come increasingly into use in common or $\frac{4}{4}$ time, as well as in $\frac{2}{4}$ and $\frac{3}{4}$, many pieces have made their appearance which could with greater convenience be notated in $\frac{12}{8}$, $\frac{9}{8}$ or $\frac{6}{8}$' [a late suggestion, but a useful one].

Of the two directions for inequality, the straightforward lengthening of the first note and shortening of the second note is a far more customary and adaptable recourse than the reversed lengthening of the second note and shortening of the first note. And lingering inequality (such as we do not find literally notated) is a much more subtle recourse than vigorous inequality (which could as well be and in fact quite often was notated by writing dotted notes). Any inequality used outside its appropriate situations, or used to an excess, can sound mannered or even grotesque. But inequality introduced at the option of the performer can be a wonderful asset in the proper places – above all, straightforward inequality in a lingering rhythm.

Dotted notes

The principle to grasp here is that in baroque notation, the ordinary dot of augmentation (which for us increases by half as much again the note preceding it) increased the note preceding it by any convenient amount. For us the length of the dot is standard, though not nearly so rigid in practice as it is in theory. For baroque notation the dot is variable. It may augment the value of the dotted note by less than half (under-dotting), by half (standard dotting), or by more than half (over-dotting), including in some cases half as much again as standard dotting (double-dotting). While double-dotting can occasionally be found notated by double dots from about the middle of the baroque period, and by tied notes from earlier, no significant difference seems to have been generally intended. As usual, the basic fact is that baroque notation was habitually casual and inconsistent to the eye, though by no means to be taken casually or inconsistently in performance. The variable dot of baroque notation is simply one more instance of this general attitude.

The evidence that the baroque dot is variable comes partly from innumerable passages of music where the notation will not add up unless it is. The situations shown in Table IV below are typical of variable dotting of this merely convenient character.

TABLE IV: The variable baroque dot

When used for deliberate expression, the variable dot has to be considered in its baroque context.

(169) Nicolas Gigault, 1683: 'When there is a semiquaver above a quaver it is necessary to take them together' [by double-dotting to synchronize a rhythmic figure, as his music shows].

(170) Michel L'Affilard, 1694: 'To perform the dots in their [intended as opposed to their notated] value, it is necessary to hold on to the dotted crotchet, and pass quickly over the following quaver.'

(171) Étienne Loulié, 1696: 'When the dot is within the same beat as the quaver which precedes it, we must hold on in singing this quaver a little longer, and pass quickly over the semiquaver which follows it.'

(172) Jacques Martin Hotteterre, 1737: 'We sometimes put dots after the notes, which augment them by half of their value'; but 'in movements where the quavers are [performed although not notated as] unequal, the dot which is after the crotchet acts as an equivalent to the dotted quaver [i.e. the dot becomes equivalent to a double dot]; in such manner that the quaver which follows a dotted crotchet is always short' [i.e. becomes equivalent to a semiquaver].

(173) Johann Mattheson, 1737: For entries and some dances it is necessary to use 'the very dotted manner'.

(174) Joachim Quantz, 1752: 'With dotted quavers, semiquavers and demisemiquavers, the standard rule is altered, for the sake of the liveliness these notes must express.' Thus 'whether in slow or quick tempo [the expression is so variable that] it is not possible to determine exactly the time of the short notes after the dot'. And 'where the dot comes after the second note' the treatment is the same 'for the length of the dot and of the first note; only the order is reversed'; and 'the shorter we perform the first' note, 'the livelier and bolder the expression; and on the contrary, the longer we make the dots, the more flattering and agreeable the expression'.

[Of what we now call French Overture style]: 'The majestic style is as much introduced with long notes, among which the other parts make a quick motion, as with dotted notes. The dotted notes must be pushed on sharply by the performer, and executed with vigour. The dot is held long, and the succeeding notes made very short.' When 'three or more demisemiquavers follow a dot or rest', such notes, 'especially in slow pieces, are not always played according to their [notated] value, but at the very end of the allotted time, and at the greatest speed; as for example often happens in overtures, entries and furies. Nevertheless, each of these quick notes must be separately bowed; and few slurs occur.' And again: 'after a long note and a short rest' demisemiquavers 'must always be played very quickly; this is so in adagio or allegro. Therefore one must wait until the very end of the time, for the quick notes, in order not to upset the balance of the measure.'

(175) C. P. E. Bach, 1753: 'The short notes following dotted notes are always performed shorter than their notation requires.' Edition of 1762: 'Since a proper accuracy is often lacking in the notation of dotted notes, a general rule of performance has become established which nevertheless shows many exceptions. According to this rule, the notes following the dot are to be performed with the greatest rapidity, and this is frequently the case. But sometimes notes in the remaining parts' require regular durations for the dots [in order to synchronize; or, conversely,] 'a feeling of smoothness impels the performer to shorten the dotted note slightly' [thus giving the same sort of approximately triplet rhythm as equally written notes prolonged by lilting inequality: a most important piece of information for expressive passages].

'Dots on long notes, likewise on short notes in slow time and also singly are usually sustained. But when many come in succession, especially in quick tempo, they are often not sustained, notwithstanding that the notation requires it [i.e. the dots are replaced by silences of articulation]. On figures where four or more short notes follow the dot, these last' must 'become sufficiently short to allow for their numerousness'.

(176) Leopold Mozart, 1756: 'In slow pieces . . . the dot has to be joined to its note with a diminuendo' and slurred to the note following; whereas 'in fast pieces . . . each note is detached from the other'.

(177) J. A. P. Schultz, 1771 (but referring to past practices): 'In the previous [i.e. the seventeenth] century, one obtained overtures from France' whence 'they first came into use. Next, they were also imitated elsewhere, particularly in Germany.' The overture is usually 'a piece of serious but fiery character in $\frac{4}{4}$ time. The motion has something lofty, the paces are slow, but adorned with many small notes' to be 'executed with fire. . . . The main notes are usually dotted, and in performance held beyond their [notated] value. After these main notes there follow more or fewer smaller' notes, 'which must be played with the utmost rapidity and so far as possible, staccato, which indeed is not practicable when 10, 12 or more notes come in one crotchet beat' [in which case they can best be taken slurred]. [N.B. for sources of French Overture style.]

Variable dotting can no more be reduced to a system than inequality. But in general:

(i) *Under-dotting may be desirable:*
If there are pairs each consisting of a dotted note and a short note, in an expressive movement; the which pairs, being neither of very long nor of very short value, might sound rather too stolid if taken

literally, but will sound agreeably lingering if taken under-dotted. The effect in these cases is to *relax* dotted notes to the same sort of approximately triplet rhythm to which equal notes can be *intensified* by lilting inequality.

If there are triplet rhythms in another part, with which dotted notes should be synchronized by under-dotting (the much rarer alternative is to over-dot instead, thereby bringing the short note not with, but decisively after the triplet).

(ii) *Standard dotting may be desirable:*

In that great majority of instances where no particular reason arises either for under-dotting or for over-dotting: it being understood that this normal situation, though standard, is not rigid, and that a little yielding this way or that will certainly arise as part of the natural shaping of the line.

In that very considerable proportion of instances where there are regular figures in another part with which dotted notes should simply be synchronized.

(iii) *Over-dotting may be desirable:*

If there are pairs each consisting of a dotted note and a short note, in an energetic movement. The degree of over-dotting is proportionate to the speed: at lower speeds double-dotting or more can be comfortably accommodated, whereas at higher speeds there is time only for slight over-dotting or for none (i.e rapid dotted pairs have probably got sufficient energy anyhow, and any attempt to over-dot them will just sound disagreeably jerky).

If there are dotted notes at twice the speed in another part, with which dotted notes written at half the speed can be synchronized by double-dotting (though they do not have to be): see *(172)* above.

As with inequality, so also there are two directions for dotted notes; and there can be an even greater flexibility of rhythm.

Straightforward dotting puts the longer note of the pair before the shorter note. In lilting rhythm approximating to triplets, the situation is just the same as lilting inequality, though reached so to speak from the opposite side (i.e. by relaxing instead of intensifying the notated rhythm). There is the same disposition to add a slur, if not already notated, and the same tendency towards a sighing fall. It is again quite possible to notate the effect intended, replacing the dotted notes by triplets indicated in the usual way, or substituting compound for simple time, as suggested by C. P. E. Bach at *(168)* above. In vigorous rhythm it is seldom desirable to add a slur; it is generally desirable to articulate the pair by making the dot, or some of the dot, almost or quite into a silence of articulation.

Reversed dotting puts the longer note of the pair after the shorter note. In lilting rhythm this approximates to lilting inequality in reverse, and likewise invites slurring and a sighing fall. In vigorous rhythm slurring is not a necessity, but it is a probability: the faster the speed, the greater the probability. Reversed dotting in any form is much more of a special effect than straightforward dotting, which in its standard rhythm is of course a commonplace in any music.

Triplet rhythms

The background here is that smaller notes can stand either in duple or in triple proportion to larger notes; and much of the purpose of mensural notation had been to indicate what proportions were intended at different levels. When we today use a triplet in binary (duple or quadruple) time, either marking it with a 3 or leaving it to be understood, we are retaining a small remnant of mensural notation; for in effect we are indicating that three of the smaller value, instead of two, go to one of the larger value. Alternatively, we can indicate, by using compound and not simple time, either that all proportions are ternary (as in $\frac{9}{8}$, which has three times three to a measure); or that a low-level proportion is ternary but a high-level proportion is binary (as in $\frac{6}{8}$, which has two times three to a measure, or in $\frac{12}{8}$, which has four times three to a measure). Our notation in these respects does not differ significantly from baroque notation.

But in one respect our practice significantly differs. During the later baroque, when the notation presents the appearance of two against three, the practice was not (as we do) to perform the cross-rhythm, but to assimilate the two rhythms one with another. This is usually done by altering the duple to fit the triple rhythm. (It is also possible under certain circumstances to alter the triple to fit the duple rhythm.)

(178) Giannantonio Banner, 1745: 'Observe in composing never to put three Notes against two, this being one of the most prohibited musical situations.' [In fact, an exaggeration by so late a date.]

What appears in the notation to be two against three can be avoided in performance by assimilating triple to duple rhythm, in one of two directions. The first note of the notated triplet can be lengthened, and the second and third notes shortened (e.g. three triplet quavers can be taken as one duplet quaver followed by two semiquavers); or the first two notes of the notated triplet can be shortened, and the third note lengthened (e.g. three triplet quavers can be taken as two duplet semiquavers followed by one quaver). Either alteration synchronizes a group of three notes with a group of

two; but though a strong case has been made out for these alterations *(179)*, they were certainly not the standard recourse.

The standard recourse for avoiding two against three in performance was by assimilating duple to triple rhythm: either lengthening the first note and shortening the second note of an equally
notated duplet (in effect a case of lilting inequality); or shortening
the dot and lengthening the following note of a duplet notated as
dotted (in effect a case of under-dotting). This is the same rhythm,
produced by different alterations of different notations, but with
identical results: duplet rhythm, as notated, assimilated to triplet
rhythm, as performed.

However, when the duplet is notated dotted, there is a further alternative, which does not assimilate duple to triple rhythm, but throws
the two rhythms into sharper contrast, thus avoiding the unwanted
ambiguity of two against three. This is not to under-dot, but to over-
dot: either indeterminately, or as double-dotting, which maximizes
the contrast and can be extremely effective in a vigorous context.

The common assimilation of duple to triple rhythm often
amounts to no more than correcting a lazy way of notating compound triple rhythm; but it can also have great expressive value.
Ordinary two against three or three against four returned to fashion
in the 'galant' music of the late baroque, and there are of course
many uncertain decisions throughout the baroque period which are
at the performer's option. Of the following examples, some concern
inequality, some concern variable dotting, some concern triplet
assimilation; but these categories are not in practice distinct. Rhythmic alteration itself is not an issue apart; it is yet another aspect of
that wider liberty by which performers were left to decide most of
the details and many of the essentials of the interpretation.

Examples of rhythmic alteration

Ex. 5. Giulio Caccini, *Nuove Musiche*, Florence, 1602, preface, brief passages
inviting inequality, with Caccini's recommendations for (a) standard, (b) reversed,
(c) free rhythm:

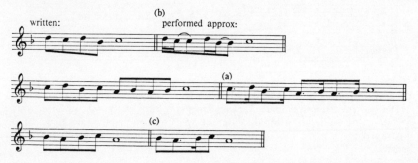

Ex. 6. Giovanni Battista Vulpio, cantata 'Dolce zampogna mia', mid-17th cent., Rome, Biblioteca Nazionale Centrale Vittorio Emanuale II, MS Musicale 162, ff. 109v–110r, many typical inconsistencies in the notation of the rhythm of matching passages requiring consistency in performance (in the instance following, the fragment of realization is original; the first option seems the best):

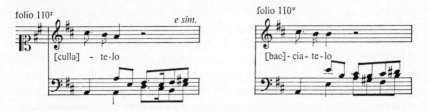

Ex. 7. 'M.r Hardel', harpsichord piece, later 17th cent., Paris, Bibl. Nat., Rés. Vm⁷. 674, f. 38, 2nd pagn.), matching quavers with inequality consistently notated in the right, inconsistently in the left hand, but inviting consistent inequality throughout:

Ex. 8. Jean Henri D'Anglebert, Sarabande grave, ed. by M. Roesgen-Champion (Paris, 1934, pp. 141 and 145) from the *Pièces de Clavecin* (Paris, 1689) and Paris, Bibl. Nat., Bauyn MS, Rés. Vm⁷, 674), m. 2, (a) in equal notation; (b) in unequal notation, representing the preferred rhythm in performance:

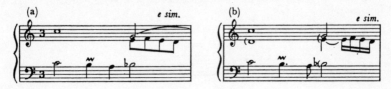

Ex. 9. Anonymous author of 'Miss Mary Burwell's Instruction Book for the Lute', c.1660–70, ed. Thurston Dart, *Galpin Society Journal*, XI, 1958, pp. 3–62, see pp. 46–7, 'demonstration for the humouring of a lesson', (a) as notated, (b) as instructed to be performed (compare the lilting inequality in Purcell at Ex. 12 below):

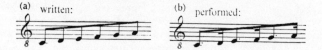

Ex. 10. Roger North, selected notes (*c.*1690) ed. John Wilson, *Roger North on Music*, London, 1959, p. 223, (b) equal (plain), (a) dotted (vigorous) and (c) triplet (lilting) rhythms as performer's options for equally notated crotchets (he writes 'it comes to the same account' in each of the following):

Ex. 11. Henry Purcell, Suite III, Almand, mm. 5–7: (a) as in Oxford, Christ Church MS 1117; (b) as in the ed. of London, 1696; and Suite IV, Corant, mm. 1–3; (c) as in Paris, Bibl. Nat., MS Rés. 1186 bis, 1; (d) as in Oxford, Ch. Ch. MS 1117; (e) as in ed. of 1696:

Ex. 12. (a) Henry Purcell, second phrase of 'Fairest Isle' (late 17th cent.), as shown in *Orpheus Britannicus*; (b) the same phrase as it is printed in *Apollo's Banquet, Second Book*, London, 1691, additional sheet, with the requisite flat notated, and also with the conventional though optional inequality notated, best taken lilting, approximately in triplet rhythm:

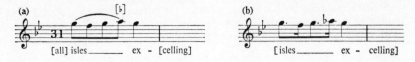

Ex. 13. Jean-Philippe Rameau, (a) *Pièces de clavecin*, Paris, 1741, Musette in E major, notated equally, but presenting a typical situation for lilting inequality, and confirmed as such by (b), unequally notated version of the same piece as the orchestral Entrée III, Scene 7 of *Les Fêtes d'Hébé*, perf. Paris, 1739 (also noteworthy are the written out upper-note preparation for the half-trill in the first full measure, and the treatment of the similarly notated ornament in m. 2 as a complete trill, a turned ending being therefore implied, and a sufficiently long upper note start being hinted in the notated appoggiatura; the appoggiaturas notated in m. 4 are on the beat, but are best taken short, and thus indistinguishable in effect from reversed inequality). The dotted notes at (b) are best under-dotted to triplet rhythms:

Just such a lilting inequality in approximately triplet rhythm may be enjoyed, for example, in the slow movement of J. S. Bach's Fourth Brandenburg Concerto (Ex. 14), since the beats comprise natural pairs moving mainly by step. Another movement which invites triplet-like inequality is the Sarabande of Bach's English Suite in A minor, where the equally notated quavers move very liltingly in triplet rhythm, though in this case the semiquavers and the occasional demisemiquavers should remain duple by reason of their speed.

But Corrette at *(166)* above quite rightly forbade inequality in such a movement as the Italian Coranto of Corelli's Violin Sonata, Op. v No. 7 (Ex. 14a), where the many leaps and considerable speed prevent either lilting or vigorous inequality from sounding agreeable. This is not a marginal case at all; it is a good example of where inequality would be misapplied and unhistorical and indeed quite inartistic. Where the case is marginal, as it very often is, equality and inequality may be one as correct as the other, and the performer is entirely at liberty to make his own choice. Where the inequality is merely required in order to read correctly a misnotation which writes equal or dotted notes with the obvious intention of their being assimilated to a prevailing triplet rhythm, then it is not really a personal choice at all, but simply a matter of knowing the appropriate convention (see Ex. 28).

Ex. 14. J. S. Bach, 4th Brandenburg Concerto, Second Movement, as it can be written out to suggest lilting inequality:

Ex. 14a. Arcangelo Corelli, Op. v No. 7, 2nd movement, not suitable for inequality:

Lully's *Amadis* (perf. Paris, 1684) had a second edition with several impressions, taken from the same plates. There are impressions in the Bibliothèque Nationale in Paris, dated 1711, 1719 and 1721. The third of these has, on pages 54–5 etc., equal notation changed in manuscript to dotted notation. On p. 74 the handwritten note appears: 'correct the middle parts of the orchestra and measure them according to the [dotted] Violins and Basses'. On pp. 75, 78, 96–7 we read 'very loud without dotting too much (*sans trop pointer*)'. On p. 108 we read: 'Equal quavers and very detached' (where they might otherwise be inequalized). On p. 118: 'Revise the Middle parts for the changes of the Measures and Value of the Notes'. On p. 139ff., under the top part: 'The sounds very firm and very detached', although here the equally notated notes are changed by hand to dotted. Conversely, at the Bibliothèque de l'Opéra, A.16.b., p. 8, m. 5 the dotted note of this print (and of the 1st ed.) has the dot scratched out by hand, and at m. 15 of the chorus 'Que le ciel annonce' has 'croches egales' written in ink; yet Lully's *Persée* (perf. Paris, 1682), Act III, prelude to Sc. iv, has in A.14.b., p. 143, the printed figure ♩ ♫ changed in ink to ♩. ♫ several times.

I take all this to hint at a very open situation, in which many passages notated equally were traditionally performed unequally (either 'not too dotted' or 'very detached' and therefore probably over-dotted); but that a conductor wishing partly otherwise in the 1721 revival of *Amadis* made his wishes known in rehearsal, from which this visible record of one particular performance (and there are others like it) comes down to us. It is this openness in the rhythmic situation which we shall do well to bear in mind today.

Ex. 15. Marin Marais, *Alcione*, perf. Paris, 1706, vigorous inequality, (a) printed short score, Paris [1706], p. 187, equal notation ('violons' and 'B.C.' shown here); (b) MS full score for revival of 1741, Paris, Bibl. Nat., Rés. Vm.[2] 205, p. 219, same passage notated dotted (as previously performed although not so notated); (c) the famous 'tempeste', Act IV, sc. iii, bass part as printed in 1706 (similar in 1741); (d) as printed for the revival of 1711; but (e) as altered in ink by (?) a contemporary conductor in the copy in the library of the Paris Opéra, A. 16, c; (f) the same copy, p. 42; as printed; (g) as altered in red crayon (many other similar cases can be found):

Ex. 16. Anon. opera (*c*.1700), Rome, Bibl. Apost. Vat., (a) score in MS Barb. lat. 4215, f. 11r, ritornello with equally notated triplets; (b) part for violins in MS Barb. lat. 4217, f. 5r, same ritornello with Siciliana rhythm notated:

Ex. 17. Alessandro Scarlatti, cantata 'Alme, voi che provaste', lilting inequality, inconsistently notated, but consistently intended, (a) in Ann Arbor, Univ. of Michigan, Stellfeld MS 1283 (*c*.1720), ff. 47–54r; (b) in Naples, Bibl. del Cons. di Mus. 'S. Pietro a Maiella', MS 34.5.5 (dated 1739), ff. 32r–37v; (c) in Florence, Baron Kraus Coll. (unnumbered, unfoliated, undated but rather late in the opinion of Edwin Hanley, who very kindly provided these examples):

Ex. 18. Domenico Scarlatti, Sonata K.491 (L.164), consistent inequality implied though inconsistently notated (choice is optional but should be kept the same throughout; similar inconsistencies of notation are numerous):

Ex. 19. J. S. Bach, 'Trauer-Ode, I' (1727; N.B.A., 1, 38, pp. 186–7), mm. 17ff., soprano solo notated equally, but shown to be intended in (lilting) inequality by the unison part for oboe d'amore notated unequally (notice that lilting inequality, rather than vigorous inequality, is suggested solely by the character of the music, since the dotted notation could serve as well for either):

Ex. 20. François Couperin; (a) *L'Apothéose de Corelli*, movt. 6 and (b) xiv Concert, prelude, m. 1, over-dotting (and at (a) one beam too many) to emphasize the great, though unmeasured, velocity:

Ex. 21. Joachim Quantz, *Essay*, Berlin, 1752, Tab. 11, Fig. 7, f, g, over-dotting for synchronization:

Ex. 22. Jean-Baptiste Lully, *Amadis*, Paris, 1684, orchestral parts in Paris, Library of Opéra, Fonds La Salle, 37, ouverture, fugal section, m. 3, (a) entry as shown in both surviving copies of B.C.; (b) as shown in bassoon part, notated differently but requiring to be synchronized:

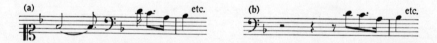

Ex. 23. G. F. Handel, autograph score, of *Jephtha*, London, Brit. Lib., R. M. 20, *e.q.* 'Ouverture', inequality needed beyond that notated in order to synchronize with notated inequality (double-dot the crotchets; dot the rests):

Ex. 24. J. S. Bach, Ouverture for harpsichord, (a) as first notated in C minor, Berlin, Deutsche Staatsbibliothek, P226, pp. 43ff., short notes shown as semiquavers; (b) as transposed by the composer for publication (Clavierübung, II, 1735) in B minor, short notes shown as demisemiquavers, i.e. approximately as they are meant to be performed in both versions alike:

Ex. 25. J. S. Bach, Fugue in D major (*Das wohltempierte Clavier*, I, 1722); (a) as notated, with rhythms written in French overture style; (b) as these rhythms may be interpreted by sharpening them in performance:

Ex. 26. George Frideric Handel, Passacaille from harpsichord suite in G minor, (a) opening best performed more or less in notated rhythm; (b) continuation as it may be notated in a modern edition so as to suggest over-dotting to the performer without imposing it upon him, and without concealing the original; (c) as it may thus be performed:

Ex. 27. Arcangelo Corelli, Op. v No. 3, Rome, 1700, Allegro, simultaneous time-signatures, (a) correctly used as a legacy of proportional notation; (b) degenerating into incorrect but convenient notation which would (see 168 above) be better and more correctly notated as at (c):

Ex. 28. George Frideric Handel, Recorder Sonata No. 4 in A minor, Larghetto, (a) as originally notated with typical baroque casualness; (b) as intended to be performed with over-dotting for assimilation to triplet rhythm (treble, m. 1) and for expression (treble, m. 6); with under-dotting for assimilation to triplet rhythm (bass, m. 1 and m. 5); and with inequality for assimilation to triplet rhythm (bass, m. 6); the whole being (see *168* above) better notated as here shown at (b), in $\frac{9}{8}$ time:

Ex. 29. J. S. Bach, Partita 1, Courante, initial up-beat note taken into the performed (unequal) rhythm of the movement itself, (a) as notated, (b) as it may be played:

Ex. 30. C. P. E. Bach, *Essay*, Berlin, 1753, III, 27: performance shown, by vertical alignment, (a) of notes notated unequally by dotting, and (b) of notes notated equally; but in performance, (a) compressed by under-dotting, and (b) expanded by inequality, to fit the rhythm of the notated triplets:

Quantz (*Essay*, Berlin, 1752, V, 22) preferred, in situations as at Ex. 30(a) above, not to under-dot, but to over-dot, thereby bringing the little note not with, but decidedly after, the last note of the triplet. Either C. P. E. Bach's recommendation or Quantz's recommendation is in such situations correct; the choice should therefore be made, by the performer, on his own judgement of which best suits the particular passage in question. (Merely standard dotted rhythm will sound feeble in such a situation, and is not to be recommended.)

Ex. 31. Georg Philipp Telemann, Gamba Sonata in A minor, (a) second movement, notated rhythm of three against four between bass and solo; (b) last movement, notated rhythm of two against three: both intended to be performed as notated:

Chapter Six · Accidentals

Accidentals inflect the line by chromatic alteration. In early baroque music they still rested to some extent with the performer, and in all baroque music they were both determined and notated by conventions considerably (though decreasingly) different from our own.

(180) Pietro Aaron, 1523: There are 'many arguments as to flats and sharps, that is whether composers should mark such accidentals'.

(181) Stephano Vanneo, 1531: For accidentals 'the ears are considered the best interpreters'.

(182) Gioseffo Zarlino, 1558: 'There are some who in singing sharpen or flatten a melody in a case which the composer never intended.'

(183) Thomas Morley, 1597: 'Because I thought it better flat than sharpe, I have set it flat. But if anie man like the other way better, let him use his discretion.' On the other hand, 'every *Cadence* [as leading note] is sharpe' [not yet quite true, but an interesting comment on the rapid decline in practice of modality].

(184) Agostino Agazzari, 1607: 'All cadences, whether intermediate or final, demand the major third [i.e. as leading note]; some people, therefore, do not mark it, but as an added precaution, I recommend using the sign.'

(185) Francesco Bianciardi, 1607: 'In the final closes, one always ends with the major Third' [i.e. as Picardy third].

(186) Crescentio Salzilli, 1611: 'One does not have to sing ♯ or ♭ except where it is marked' [but still one may].

(187) Domenico Mazzocchi, 1638 (an unusually punctilious composer in his notation): [Chromatic] 'alterations are not to be made, unless they are found marked; excepting, however, the notes immediately following on the same degree', which remain 'until another new sign is found'.

(188) Wolfgang Ebner, 1653: 'When it is a full cadence, the last note must always be taken with the sharp' [Picardy third].

(189) Christopher Simpson, 1665: A flat or a sharp 'serves only for that particular Note before which it is placed' [the basic baroque rule in spite of very many exceptions]. 'That ♭ takes away a *Semitone* from the Sound of the Note before which it is set, to make it more *grave* or *flat*: This ♯ doth add a semitone to the Note to make it more *acute* or *sharp*' [the basic baroque convention].

(190) Lorenzo Penna, 1672: 'On the last note', a 'major third' [Picardy third].

(191) Friedrich Erhard Niedt, 1700: Close in the major [Picardy third], except that 'French composers do the opposite', not necessarily for the best.

(192) Étienne Loulié, 1696: 'The sharp is marked thus, ♯, and raises the note by a semitone. The flat is marked thus, ♭, and lowers the note by a semitone. The natural is marked thus, ♮, and removes a flat' or 'a sharp. A Sharp or a Flat put before a Note, serves also for all those which follow immediately on the same Degree.'
[MS Supplément:] 'Some Italians and other' foreigners 'use a ♮ after a ♯ to indicate that the note' thus marked 'is natural again. . . . Among the Italians: A sharp raises a note a semitone higher than a natural. A note is lowered a semitone beneath a natural by means of a flat. A note is made natural by means of a ♮' [these are transitional features].

(193) Francesco Geminiani, 1751: 'A Sharp (♯) raises the Note to which it is prefixed, a Semitone higher. . . . A Flat (♭) on the Contrary renders the Note to which it is prefixed, a Semitone lower [as in Simpson at *189* above]. This Mark (♮) takes away the Force of both the Sharp and the Flat and restores the Note before which it is placed to its natural Quality' [not in Simpson at *189*, and nearer to our own system].

(194) Daniel Gottlob Türk, 1789: Accidentals 'are valid only through one bar; yet one must not wish to observe this rule too strictly, for such a modifying sign often remains valid through several bars, or indeed so long, until it is cancelled by a ♮. [Moreover:] One still finds now and again, especially among the French and in older works, pieces in which a ♯ stands in place of our sharpening ♮' and '♭ for a flattening ♮'. [The transition to our modern system still in progress: it was not fully accomplished until well into the nineteenth century.]

Placement or displacement by accidentals

A modern accidental *places* a note, by giving it an absolute position within the tonal system. But a baroque accidental *displaces* a note, by giving it a position relative to that which it would otherwise have had. (See *189*, *192*, *193* and *194* above.) That is the radical distinction of which a modern editor most needs to be aware.

The ♮ sign, originally the 'hard' or natural B as opposed to the 'soft' or flat B, was still used in early baroque music chiefly in that historic capacity, i.e. to restore B natural but (in theory) no other note: hence ♯ and ♭ did double duty, until the growing use (perhaps earliest in Italy) of ♮ for cancellation freed ♯ and ♭ for the single duty to which they are confined today.

Let us suppose that a baroque musician wants to inflect B flat to B natural: he sets a ♯ to rise a semitone, and calls it 'sharped', as Ex. 32a below. For him, G major has a 'sharp third' and is therefore a 'sharp key'. Thus what looks like B sharp notates B natural: Ex. 32a below. He wants to inflect B sharp to B natural: he sets a ♭ to drop a semitone, and calls it 'flatted', as in Ex. 32b. For him, G sharp minor has a 'flat third' and is a 'flat key'. Here, what looks like B flat notates B natural: Ex. 32b. He wants to inflect C flat to C natural: he sets a ♯ to rise a semitone, and calls it 'sharped', as in Ex. 32c. He wants to inflect C sharp to C natural: he sets a ♭ to drop a semitone, and calls it 'flatted', as in Ex. 32d. In the one case, what looks like C sharp notates C natural; in the other case, what looks like C flat also notates C natural. He wants to restore B double-flat to B flat: he sets a ♯, as in Ex. 32e; what looks like B sharp notates B flat. He wants to restore C double-sharp to C sharp: he sets a ♭, as at Ex. 32f; what looks like C flat notates C sharp. (But equally he might set nothing in the notation to restore double-flat to flat, or double-sharp to sharp; or again, he might just set a flat or a sharp, as we might often do; but only the context can tell us what was his intention.)

Ex. 32g and Ex. 32h below are common and Ex. 32i and Ex. 32j are uncommon types of baroque notation. Ex. 32k and Ex. 32l show rare uses (but found in Leclair) of ♮ to restore a previously cancelled ♯ or ♭; Ex. 32m (J. P. Treiber, *Der accurate Organist*, Jena, 1704, Ex. xii) and Ex. 32n (Alfonso Ferrabosco, in Oxford, Ch. Ch. MS 2, f248v, m.36) show fairly common types of enharmonic substitution. Not all our problems over baroque accidentals are as daunting as this, and most modern editors will have taken reasonably good care of them. But it is important to know what uncertainties may arise, not only because mistakes are always possible, but also because the choice may sometimes be at the performer's option.

Ex. 32. Accidentals altering but not defining a note:

Persistence of accidentals

A modern accidental, unless cancelled by a sign, persists through the measure, and unless tied across, is then cancelled by the bar-line. But a baroque accidental affects, in principle, only that note to which it is attached, and the bar-line has no effect upon it either way. (See *186, 187, 189, 192* and *194*.)

In practice, there were many inconsistencies. Peri *(195)* was probably being a little pedantic in wanting an accidental to affect 'that note alone on which it is shown, even though there may be several repetitions of that note'; and certainly he was quite inconsistent in his own notation with regard to this (see Ex. 33 below). Mazzocchi, who was on the whole punctilious, conceded immediate repetitions as being still affected, though he too was inconsistent in his own notation (see *187* and Ex. 34).

Repetitions of the same note separated by a rest, or still more by the start of a new phrase, or both, were not generally taken to be affected by the accidental unless the sign for it was renewed; but inconsistencies are again very usual. Repetition with one or two other notes intervening might or might not be taken as still affected. (See Ex. 34 and Ex. 36.)

The influence of an accidental (particularly of a flat) in early baroque music is more likely to persist while the phrase remains within the compass of the prevailing hexachord. A hexachord is a six-note segment of diatonic scale such that it only includes one semitone, and always in the middle between the notes at the moment deemed to be mi and fa. To exceed or inflect this was deemed to be mutating into another hexachord. (See Table v and Ex. 44 and Ex. 45.)

The following considerations may be helpful in some cases of uncertainty.

Sequences, matching passages and fugal textures are particularly liable to imply, for the sake of symmetry, a more consistent use of accidentals than their notation always indicates. Unless modal influence to the contrary is to be given precedence, it is usually best to supply whatever accidentals are necessary to round out the pattern.

Some notated accidentals appear to be cautionary, adding nothing to what is already implied or stated by the remainder of the notation. They may give useful confirmation, or alternatively they may be somewhat mystifying if they are themselves inconsistent or ambiguous – or even, of course, mistaken: a possibility always to be taken into account. The fact that one note is given a notated accidental, whether cautionary or otherwise, while another note which seems neither more nor less eligible for one is not, counts for little: we must not infer that the difference in notation necessarily indicates a difference of intention. It is just as likely to be a purely casual discrepancy, handing it over to us to make our performer's decision on the usual grounds of taste and context. If the context is unmistakably modal, it is essential to apply the necessary knowledge; on the other hand, mode hardly affected the greater part of baroque music in practice after the earlier years, and except in certain ecclesiastical situations where a stricter attitude prevailed. If

TABLE V

The hexachordal system

Pitch in Helmholtz's notation	HARD HEX'D*	NAT'L HEX'D†	SOFT HEX'D‡	HARD HEX'D*	NAT'L HEX'D†	SOFT HEX'D‡	HARD HEX'D*	THE BASIC GAMUT
e''							E *la*	E *la* (Ela)
d''						D *la*	D *sol*	D *la sol* (Delasol)
Treble c''						C *sol*	C *fa*	C *sol fa* (Cesolfa)
b'						b *fa* B		b *fa* B (Befa) *mi* or *mi*
							B *mi* B	B (Bemi)
a'					A *la*	A *mi*	A *re*	A *la mi re* (Alamire)
g'					G *sol*	G *re*	G *ut*	G *sol re ut* (Gesolreut)
f'					F *fa*	F *ut*		F *fa ut* (Fefaut)
e'				E *la*	E *mi*			E *la mi* (Elami)
d'			D *la*	D *sol*	D *re*			D *la sol re* (Delasolre)
Middle c'			C *sol*	C *fa*	C *ut*			C *sol fa ut* (Cesolfaut)
bb			b *fa* B					b *fa* B (Befa) *mi* or *mi*
b♮				B *mi* B				B (Bemi)
a		A *la*	A *mi*	A *re*				A *la mi re* (Alamire)
g		G *sol*	G *re*	G *ut*				G *sol re ut* (Gesolreut)
f		F *fa*	F *ut*					F *fa ut* (Fefaut)
e	E *la*	E *mi*						E *la mi* (Elami)
d	D *sol*	D *re*						D *sol re* (Desolre)
Tenor C	C *fa*	C *ut*						C *fa ut* (Cafaut)
B	B *mi* B							B *mi* (Bemi)
A	A *re*							A *re* (Are)
G	Γ *ut*							Γ *ut* (Gamma Ut)

* *Hexachordum durum*, because it includes *b durum* or *quadration*, i.e. B *mi* (B natural).

† *Hexachordum naturale*, including no B.

‡ *Hexachordum molle*, because it includes B *molle* or *rotundum*, i.e. b *fa* (B flat).

in doubt, consult an expert. If not, consult your judgement, but do not hesitate to take the matter well in hand.

Ordinary key tonality – much the commonest situation – shows especially at cadences, whether slight or substantial. Thus the seventh of the scale, taken as leading note on a bass moving from fifth to tonic, is normally taken sharp whether so notated or not; when the seventh is preceded or followed by the sixth of the scale, this also is normally taken sharp whether so notated or not. Otherwise an improbable augmented second comes between (not an unknown interval by expressive intention, but never meant by mere casual inadvertence: a fact so obvious then that the notated accidental is much more commonly assumed but missing on the sixth than it is on the seventh). Except where modal tonality intervenes, it may be regarded as almost certain that the seventh of the scale as leading note, and the sixth of the scale if present in support of it, are to be taken sharp – or, which comes to the same effect, are to be taken natural if they would otherwise be flat. (Exx. 55–8 and Ex. 60.)

There is, of course, a melodic as well as a harmonic disposition towards the sharp sixth and seventh, and especially towards arriving at the tonic from the leading note across the easy interval of the semitone. The same inclination towards the easiest progression perhaps accounts for another convention far older than key tonality. This was expressed in hexachordal terms by the late-medieval tag, still evoked in theory and practice through the renaissance and even up to a point the baroque period: 'Una nota super la Semper est canendum fa' (One note above la is always to be sung fa). Now the interval from la to fa is in hexachordal organization necessarily a semitone wherever it may be deemed to occur. If the top of a phrase goes up by one step and down again by one step, with no other notes intervening, then this step however notated is to be taken flat, i.e. as a semitone. Conversely, by a corresponding but much less regular and dependable convention, if the bottom of a phrase goes down by one step and up again by one step, with no other notes intervening, then that step however notated may not improbably be taken sharp, i.e. as a semitone. As with the leading note, melodic and harmonic considerations may perhaps be found colluding here. (Ex. 68 and Ex. 69.)

The tritone, whether as augmented fourth or as diminished fifth, had long ago been disparaged under another medieval tag: 'Tritonus est diabolus in musica' (The tritone is the devil in music). The objection was certainly not to the quite mild dissonance of this interval, but to its extreme ambivalence within the tonal field: it cuts the octave exactly in half and can take either direction or none. As melody or as harmony, there is no interval like the tritone for sitting tonally on the fence. It was indeed very poignantly exploited by such revolutionaries as Monteverdi and others at the start of the baroque period: modulations were built on the tritone relationship that were little other than harmonic side-steps, very effective in certain dramatic contexts. In disguise, the tritone underlies that subsequently fashionable progression, the Neapolitan Sixth; but the classical generation of Alessandro Scarlatti and Corelli was far more intolerant of tonal ambiguity. Tritones as melody passed well enough, but tritones as harmony remained so suspect that a fifth in figured bass, for example, was assumed to be perfect without needing an accidental to notate it so in the figuring (Ex. 70).

The Middle Ages disliked any final third, as sounding less definitive than bare fifths and octaves. The renaissance disliked minor final thirds, perhaps because they clash subliminally but restlessly with the major third unavoidably present above the fundamental in the acoustic resonance of the harmonic series: final thirds were therefore made major, where necessary, by the unwritten convention sometimes known as the Picardy Third. This persisted into the baroque period at any rate for figured bass (as at *185* and *188* above), though with certain reservations *(191)*. (See also Ex. 71 and Ex. 72 below.)

There are altogether more performer's options over baroque accidentals than has been until recently appreciated. They do need, however, a practised ear and considerable caution. We do not always have to assume that only one solution is acceptable.

Examples involving accidentals

Ex. 33. Jacopo Peri, *Euridice*, 1600, (a) p. 34, m. 17; (b) p. 36, m. 16; (c) p. 54, m. 13; inconsistent accidentals; departing from his rule at (a) and (c).

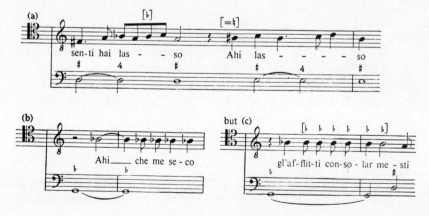

Ex. 34. Domenico Mazzocchi, *Partitura de' madrigali*, Rome, 1638, (a) pp. 63–74, 'Pian piano', m. 17; (b) pp. 52–62, 'Oh se potreste mai', m. 22, inconsistent accidentals; at (a) superfluous to his rule; at (b) cautionary after rest:

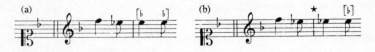

Ex. 35. [? Luigi Rossi], oratorio, *Un peccator pentito mi son fatto nemico* (mid-17th cent.), (a) in Rome, Vatican Lib., Barb. Lat. 4191, f. 13v, accidental notated once; (b) in Rome, Vatican Lib., Barb. Lat. 4201, f. 84v, the same accidental notated twice, perhaps because the page turns over in between (at*):

Ex. 36. Giacomo Carissimi, cantata, 'In un mar di pensieri' (mid-17th cent.), m. 12, (a) in London, Brit. Lib. R.M. 24. i. 11, No. 5; (b) in Vienna, Österreichische Nationalbibliothek, MS 17765; (c) in Oxford, Christ Church Lib., MS 51; same accidentals differently notated:

But in Ex. 37, the musical sense depends upon a chromatic sequence which *precludes* carrying the influence of the accidentals forward over the notes in between, whether cancelling accidentals are notated, as at (b), or not, as at (a).

Ex. 37. J. S. Bach, 'Coffee Cantata', autograph MS, Berlin, Preussische Staatsbibliothek (c.1732), (a) p. 10, m. 5; (b) p. 11, m. 10; inconsistent accidentals:

At Ex. 38, the first two Ds in Tenor 11 are sharp, as leading notes in a normal ornamental resolution of the suspended E. But the third D is not a leading note. It is the start of a new phrase, and is therefore no longer under the influence of the previous accidental. This is confirmed by the lute tablature, which shows the fingering for D natural, and also by the need to avoid an improbably augmented second to the C natural next following.

Ex. 38. John Dowland, *Lachrimae*, London [1605], 'Lachrimae Verae', m. 22, influence of accidental cancelled by start of new phrase, though the note is immediately repeated.

At Ex. 39, the first G is correctly marked sharp as the leading note of A minor; but the next G is the start of a new phrase, and is therefore no longer under the influence of the previous accidental. It is G natural, as the harmony confirms by progressing into C major.

Ex. 39. Giacomo Carissimi, cantata, 'Deh, memoria' (mid-17th cent.), in Rome, Vatican Lib., MS Chigi Q. iv. 18, ff. 43–8v, and also in Rome, Vatican Lib., MS Chigi Q. iv. 11, ff. 1–6v, m. 29; influence of accidental cancelled by start of new phrase (rather than by the one different note in between, and certainly not by the bar-line):

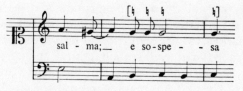

In Ex. 40, the first phrase is in D minor, with the leading note and the sixth of the scale both sharpened. The second phrase is in F major, which confirms that the C which starts it after the rest is natural.

Ex. 40. John Jenkins, 'Fantasia 21', Treble 1, in London, Brit. Lib. MS Add. 17192 (mid-17th cent.), f. 50; influence of accidental cancelled by rest and start of new phrase.

Ex. 41. Claudio Monteverdi, *Orfeo*, perf. Mantua, 1607, pub. Venice, 1609, Act II, violin parts in the aria 'Possente spirto', sharp in ascent not influencing subsequent descent:

Ex. 42. Antonio Vivaldi, violin concerto in A minor, Op. 3 (*L'Estro armonico*, Amsterdam, 1712), No. 6, 1st movt., m. 55, solo violin, ascending sharps not influencing subsequent descent in a minor melody:

Ex. 43 shows the first B marked natural, as sharpened leading note to C minor. The second and third Bs go better flat; but the first A still goes better natural, as sixth of the minor scale sharpened in ascent. The second and third As, being in descent, go better flat. The first D goes rather better natural, as perfect fifth of a G major triad; and so it is marked for the sequence an octave lower in m. 84. The second D (in m. 82) may well remain natural, and is so marked in m. 84. But in m. 82, not only the first but the second and third Bs are marked natural, the first A is marked natural, the second A (in m. 83) is marked flat: a more striking (though not necessarily better) solution because of the augmented second from m. 82 to m. 83; but at a first reading you could not see that coming. In m. 85, the first B must be taken natural, retrospectively from the marked B natural following, or simply as sharpened leading note to the dominant seventh. Add to this that Trevor Pinnock in course of a most valuable discussion cited an earlier manuscript (Manchester Central Library) used by him, which shows the first D of m. 82 marked flat (suggesting D natural in m. 81), no accidental in m. 83, and the first D of m. 84 natural but the second flat; so how, we asked, can any *one* right solution possibly emerge from such a typically inconsistent state of the evidence? The whole moral is that the performer chooses.

Ex. 43. Antonio Vivaldi, *Il cimento dell' armonia e dell' inventione*, Op. 8, Paris and Amsterdam [both *c.*1730], 'The four seasons', etc., No. 4, 'Winter', 3rd movt., mm. 80–5, inconsistently notated accidentals:

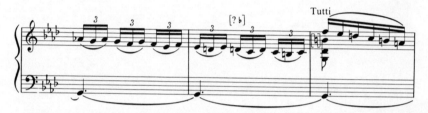

In Ex. 44, the compass remains that of the hard hexachord from G *sol re ut* to E *la mi*, and the influence of the B natural persists, as the marked B natural in Treble 1 confirms.

Ex. 44. John Dowland, *Lachrimae*, London [1605], 'M. Giles Hobies Galiard', m. 21, continued influence of accidental within the compass of one hexachord (lower part):

In Ex. 45(a), the piece begins in D minor (to us), with notated C sharp (as leading note) and B flat (as descending sixth of the scale). The presumption (to a baroque musician) was therefore the untransposed soft hexachord. The first B in the right hand has no accidental notated, but is by hexachordal tendency a flat, like the next B, which is notated flat. (To us, the tonality is F major, with the same implication.) At m. 10, the melody exceeds the compass of a hexachord, and the B is natural. This is confirmed by the need to avoid an improbable (in this context, impossible) augmented second from the notated C sharp immediately before.

In Ex. 45(b), the hexachordal tendency is to keep the second B as a B flat; but this tendency is overcome by the stronger tendency to take it as the leading note to C, and therefore natural.

Ex. 45. Anonymous keyboard pieces from the Gresse MS (17th-cent. Dutch), in *Dutch Keyboard Music of the 16th and 17th Centuries*, ed. Alan Curtis, Amsterdam, 1961, (a) p. 108, LXXX, 'Menuets du Dauphin', mm. 4–10; influence of flat prevailing because of the soft hexachord; (b) p. 100, LXIX, 'Courante', mm. 4–5, influence of flat not prevailing:

In Ex. 46, the bass note E has a sharp above it to indicate the major third, G sharp, thus showing that the sharp before the second G in the melody is retrospective, influencing also the first G in the melody.

Ex. 46. Jacopo Peri, *Euridice*, Florence, 1600, p. 14, m. 13, retrospective accidental:

In Ex. 47, the bass note A is preceded by a sharp in the C space a third above, which is a common placing in very early figured bass for an accidental showing the major or the minor third as harmony. Cantus I sounds D against the E in Cantus II, and against the C sharp thus shown in the accompaniment; this D resolves ornamentally on to C sharp (i.e. the dissonance D is sounded together with its note of resolution C sharp, a progression favoured in early baroque though not in later baroque practice). The C sharp in the accompaniment confirms that in Cantus I the first C, which is not marked, must be sharp, as well as the second C, which is marked. The sharp which is marked against the second C in Cantus I must therefore be exerting a retrospective as well as a prospective influence.

Ex. 47. Lodovico (Grossi da) Viadana, *Cento concerti ecclesiastici*, Venice, 1602, IV, 'Laetare Hierusalem', m. 3 (of bass):

In Ex. 48, at (a), the sharp before the second G in Treble 1 is retrospective, influencing also the first G; this is confirmed by the lute tablature, which shows the fingering for G sharp on both notes. But at (b), a very interesting passage, the sharp before the last G in Treble 1 is not retrospective, and does not influence the G immediately preceding it; this is confirmed by the harmony, by the coincident G natural in Tenor 1, and by the lute tablature.

Ex. 48. John Dowland, *Lachrimae*, London [1605], 'Lachrimae Amantis', (a) m. 3, retrospective accidental; (b) mm. 9–11, accidental not retrospective.

In Ex. 49, (a) and (b) are from the aria 'Possente spirto', in which Monteverdi has notated two alternative versions: the upper is left plain enough for the singer to ornament at will; the lower is already much ornamented and needs little if any further ornamentation. At (a), the first sharp in the lower version is retrospective, as the upper version seems to confirm. At (b), the first sharp in the lower version is normally retrospective, but exceptionally interesting in being joined by a tie; the remaining sharps are erratically notated, but all the Fs are sharp, both as leading notes and by hexachordal tendency; the upper version has no Fs. At (c), which is a duet, the sharps in either voice are retrospective, and the sharp in the upper voice is persistent, both as leading note and by hexachordal tendency.

Ex. 49. Claudio Monteverdi, *Orfeo*, perf. Mantua, 1607, pub. Venice, 1609, (a) f. 56, m. 5, and (b) f. 58, m. 7, Act III, aria, 'Possente spirto', (c) f. 95, m. 7, Act V, duet, 'Saliam cantand' al Cielo'; accidentals retrospective and persisting.

At Ex. 50(a), the first F in m. 2 of the lower voice is notated sharp; but the second F, which is not given an accidental, must be taken natural, since it is plainly the tonic of an F major triad, in root position, with the F natural an octave below already sounding in the bass.

At Ex. 50(b), the first C in the second part from the top would, other things being equal, probably be best taken sharp by retrospective influence from the second C, which, as leading note, is (correctly) notated sharp; the B before being then taken natural as sixth of the scale. But other things are not equal; for the first C is plainly functioning as the fifth (i.e. the dominant) in a six-three inversion of an F major triad (the D which persists in the lower part but one becoming an 'added sixth' to this inverted triad). We therefore know here that the sharp notated is not retrospective.

Ex. 50. Claudio Monteverdi, *Orfeo*, perf. Mantua, 1607, pub. Venice, 1609, (a) Act v, accidental proved by the harmony not to persist; (b) Act III, accidental proved by the harmony not to be retrospective:

Ex. 51. Lodovico (Grossi da) Viadana, *Cento concerti ecclesiastici*, Venice, 1602, II, 'Peccavi super numerum', m. 10 (counting by the bass), cautionary accidental to *prevent* retrospective influence:

Ex. 52. Claudio Monteverdi, *Orfeo*, perf. Mantua 1607, pub. Venice 1609, p. 45, mm. 7–8 (Act II), two cautionary accidentals at the bass B flat and the 1st tenor C natural (and one more needed which is conspicuous by its absence at the 2nd tenor G natural):

Ex. 53 shows a cautionary sharp (i.e. natural) against two Es which would need no such precaution were it not that a baroque musician would otherwise have taken them as obvious cases of *Una nota super la Semper est canendum fa:* i.e. as E flats.

Ex. 53. Claudio Monteverdi, *Orfeo*, perf. Mantua, 1607, pub. Venice 1609, Act II, duet, cautionary sharps notated to prevent an improvised flattening on single notes rising to and falling from the top of a phrase:

Ex. 54. J[an Pieterszoon]. S[weelinck?]., 'Praeludium', LXXI in *Dutch Keyboard Music of the 16th and 17th Centuries*, ed. Alan Curtis from the Gresse MS (17th-cent. Dutch), Amsterdam, 1961, p. 101, matching phrase transferred from right hand to left hand, and therefore probably requiring matching accidentals (added editorial accidental is mine):

In Ex. 55 below, at (a) the G in the voice part requires a sharp to match its imitation by the bass in the same measure; and this is confirmed by this G sharp serving momentarily as leading note to the A. The two As in the bass need a sharp third figured. At (b), the C requires a sharp to be consistent with (a). At (c), the two Cs, the F and the G in the voice part, and the C in the bass, all require sharps to be consistent with (a). The two As in the bass again require a sharp third figured. At (d), the two Fs and the C in the voice part require sharps, and the bass requires a sharp third figured, to be consistent with (b). The only other source at present known (Naples, Bibl. del Conservatorio di Musica 'S. Pietro a Majella', MS 33.4.17 II, ff.

145–56) is virtually identical with the source quoted, and shows no variants in this passage.

Ex. 55. Giacomo Carissimi, cantata, 'Apretivi, inferni' (mid-17th cent.), in Modena, Bibl. Estense, MS Mus. G. 32 (a separate MS, dated 1662), (a) mm. 95–6; (b) m. 104, corresponding passage; (c) mm. 153–4, section corresponding to (a) in the written-out da capo repetition; (d) m. 165, passage corresponding to (b) – all requiring consistent accidentals:

Ex. 56. Giacomo Carissimi, solo cantata, 'Bel tempo per me se n' andò' (mid-17th cent.), Rome, Vatican Lib., MS Barb. lat. 4136, ff. 43–52 (identical for these passages in Bologna, Conservatory, MS X234, ff. 69–76v), (a) sharpened leading note required though not marked; (b) matching passage confirming this by marking the required sharp (the rhythm should also be kept consistent, i.e. dotted):

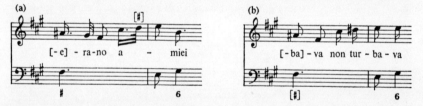

Ex. 57. Claudio Monteverdi, *Orfeo*, perf. Mantua, 1607, pub. Venice, 1609, Act I, sixth of the scale requiring to be sharpened where the seventh of the scale is sharpened as leading note:

Ex. 58. Jean-Philippe Rameau, *Castor et Pollux*, Paris, 1737, (a) printed score, accidental requiring to be supplied on the sixth of the scale rising to the correctly sharpened seventh of the scale as leading note; (b) confirmation from the same accidental correctly notated in the 'Basse Continuë Generalle', Paris, Bibl. Nat. Vm² 335:

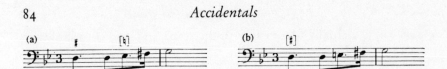

That Ex. 58 shows a genuine instance of old-fashioned notation, rather than a mere slip of the pen, is perhaps rather confirmed by the occurrence of other, unmistakable archaisms. Thus in the surviving manuscript part-books for the same opera (the set is not complete), both sharp and natural signs are used for cancelling flats in the signature, evidently with no distinction intended, as at Ex. 59.

Ex. 59. Jean-Philippe Rameau, *Castor et Pollux* (printed Paris, 1737), manuscript part-book, Paris, Bibl. Nat. Vm² 335, (a) 'S⁴ Violon D'acc. [concertino] hautbois et flûte', chorus 'C'est à toi', m. 7, sharp sign used to cancel flat in signature; (b) one copy of 'Sᵉ Violin [ripieno]', ibid., playing the same notes in unison, natural sign used to cancel flat in signature (another copy of this ripieno part, however, is notated like the concertino part):

Ex. 60. John Dowland, *Lachrimae*, London, [1605], 'Lachrimae Coactae', m. 2, sixth note of the scale requiring to be sharpened when the seventh note is sharp as leading note (the minim F natural should I think be shortened to a crotchet, since it would otherwise clash unmeaningfully against the necessarily sharpened sixth above it; and such careless note-lengths at phrase-endings are common enough):

In Ex. 61, m. 2, the alto enters (and is correctly and meaningfully shown as entering) on a G natural against the G sharp correctly shown (as leading note) in the treble. The F in the alto is also correctly shown as natural; but the ornamental resolution in m. 3 of the lute tablature (here transcribed into staff notation) correctly shows F sharp as the sixth of the scale to the correctly sharpened G as the seventh of the scale. Thus the solution here, bold as it may appear, is simply to follow the notated accidentals as written, with no editorial modification whatsoever.

Ex. 61. John Dowland, *Lachrimae*, London, [1605], 'Lachrimae Antiquae', concluding measures, accidentals as notated bold but correct:

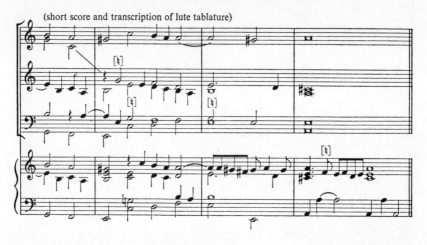

(short score and transcription of lute tablature)

At Ex. 62(a), the second measure shows a clearly notated augmented second from E flat to F sharp; and others as clear occur
elsewhere in *Orfeo* to emphasize words of grief or compassion. We
might possibly though by no means certainly take the influence of
the sharp as extending to the other Fs, which gives matching augmented seconds, as here optionally suggested.

At Ex. 62(b), the diminished third is confirmed by the bass, of
which the tritone progression (also found elsewhere in *Orfeo*) is in
turn confirmed by the melody: the words are grievous enough to
warrant it.

At Ex. 62(c), the clearly notated augmented second is again
warranted by the grievous words.

At Ex. 62(d), on the other hand, the words are happy, and the
shape of the melody discourages an augmented second.

Ex. 62. Claudio Monteverdi, *Orfeo*, perf. Mantua, 1607, pub. Venice, 1609, (a) Act
III, harp obbligato in the aria 'Possente spirto', (b) Act IV, (c) Act V, unusual but
correct melodic intervals; (d) Act V, usual interval correct:

(a)

Ex. 63. Giovanni Coperario (John Cooper), fantasy 'Che Pue Mirarvi' [sic] (early 17th cent.), Christ Church Lib., Oxford, MS 21, m. 5 on p. 163 (no variant accidentals here in Christ Church, MS 2, f. 170v; the parts move naturally to produce the clash; and the idiom is both typical and beautiful):

Ex. 64. Nicholas Carleton, 'Gloria Tibi Trinitas', Mulliner MS (English, 2nd half of 16th cent.), ed. Denis Stevens, *Musica Britannica*, I, London, 1951, p. 5 (rarer thus, but not very rare):

Ex. 65. Claudio Monteverdi, *Orfeo*, perf. Mantua, 1607, pub. Venice, 1609, Act v, diminished octave approached by leap (a much harsher variant, but Monteverdi often does it):

Ex. 66. John Blow, passages quoted by Dr Burney *(196)* as unacceptable, but certainly intended by Blow:

In examples such as those above, harmonies or progressions which are, to some extent, exceptional are nevertheless correct, and no changes of the notated accidentals is required or acceptable.

But in other instances, a change in the notated accidentals may be required or at least desirable, simply because the harmony or the progression itself suggests it. With every precaution against making anachronistic changes, we should nevertheless take these harmonic considerations into account, even where none of the practices so far discussed seems quite to cover them. In the following, both reasons coincide.

Ex. 67. William Randall, setting of Dowland's 'Lachrimae Pavan', in *Tisdale's Virginal Book*, c.1600, ed. Alan Brown, London, 1966, pp. 17–22, (a) m. 6, E flat correctly notated in bass; (b) mm. 13–16, corresponding passage, E flat in bass, etc., correctly added in bass by the editor (correct as harmony and also as *una nota super la*, one note rising to the top of its phrase and falling):

Ex. 68. (a) Henry Purcell, second phrase of 'Fairest Isle' (late 17th cent.), as shown in *Orpheus Britannicus*, one note rising and at once falling again at the top of the phrase, and therefore requiring to be taken flat although not so marked here or in most copies; (b) the same phrase as it is printed in *Apollo's Banquet, Second Book*, London, 1691, additional sheet, with the requisite flat notated, and also with the conventional though optional inequality notated, for which see Chapter v above; (c) Giacomo Carissimi, 'Amor mio', Bologna, Civico Museo Bibliografico Musicale, MS v 289, ff. 139–42v, m. 7 on f. 140v (and identically here in Harvard Univ., Houghton Lib., MS Mus. 106; Modena, Biblioteca Estense, MS Mus. G. 30; Venice, Conservatorio di Musica, MS 11), one note rising and falling again at the top of the phrase, and therefore requiring to be taken flat although not so marked:

Ex. 69. Jean-Baptiste Lully, *Amadis*, Paris, 1684, Act v, 'Chaconne', bass requiring an added flat (for the single note rising and falling at the top of the phrase) confirmed on harmonic grounds (to conform with the prevailing key of C minor):

In Ex. 70 (a), in one manuscript the A is notated as natural, though both melodic and harmonic considerations may incline us to take this as A flat, including the expressive diminished fourth from A flat to E. We can confirm our inclination, not only from matching passages in the same piece, but from the same passage in another manuscript, which notates A flat, as at (b). A similar case, confirmed by a matching passage, is shown at (c) and (d). The tritones here are in strict parallel and must therefore both be right.

Ex. 70. Giacomo Carissimi, (a) 'In un mar di pensieri' (mid-17th cent.), London, King's Music Lib. (Brit. Lib.), MS R.M. 24. i. 11, No. 5, m. 52, diminished fourth requiring to be introduced though not so notated; (b) the same passage in Vienna, Österreichische Nationalbibliothek, MS 17765, ff. 41–8v, showing the required accidental notated; (c) same piece, Brit. Lib. MS R.M. 24. i. m. 68, melodic tritone requiring to be introduced although not so notated; (d) m. 74, confirmation from matching passage so notated:

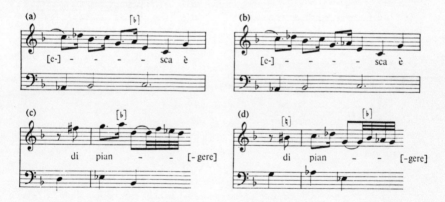

Ex. 71 shows a normal dominant to tonic passing close, from E major triad to A major triad. It is, I think, necessary to supply editorially a sharp on the two Gs, although none appears in the notation. For the sharp supplied editorially on F, and for the sharp supplied editorially as a figuring of the bass A (rendering this unmarked triad major instead of minor), see p. 72 above.

Ex. 71. Claudio Monteverdi, *Orfeo*, perf. Mantua, 1607, pub. Venice, 1609, Act I, duet, leading note G unmarked but requiring to be sharpened (also sixth of scale F unmarked but requiring to be sharpened; also Picardy Third, unmarked but required in the accompaniment):

Ex. 72. Giacomo Carissimi, 'Deh, memoria' (mid-17th cent.), in Rome, Vatican Lib., (a) MS Chigi Q. IV. 18, ff. 43–8v, m. 88, voice-part entering in the minor immediately after the Picardy Third in the major, with no cautionary accidental to alert the singer, and none needed for a baroque singer; (b) the same MS at m. 79, cautionary accidental in the figuring of the bass, to prevent a Picardy Third otherwise sure to be introduced by a baroque accompanist; (c) the same measure MS Chigi Q. IV. 11, ff. 1–6v, Picardy Third notated in the figuring of the bass, by a scribe evidently preferring it that way:

Chapter Seven · Ornamenting the Line

Choice and necessity

Baroque ornamentation is more than a decoration. It is a necessity.
It is of course a very fluid necessity; but there has to be enough of it
and of the right kinds.

Inheriting as it did from the renaissance an ancient tradition of
free ornamentation, and adding to this freedom a comparatively
novel growth of small, specific ornaments, baroque ornamentation
took on a complexity by no means the whole of which can be
dependably reconstructed now. Our difficulty here is that the surviving evidence, though abundant, is full of ambiguities. It can be
very rewarding to explore the more complicated and uncertain
possibilities; but the relatively simple selection of ornaments
presented in this book is probable sufficient for most ordinary
situations. It is, indeed, indispensable.

From about the middle of the baroque period, two situations
particularly required free ornamentation in order to complete the
design intended. One is the more or less improvised variation of the
repeated first section in da capo arias. The other is the more or less
improvised melody, for which only the supporting harmony-notes
may be notated, in many slow movements by such composers as
Corelli or Handel. In addition, certain contexts implied a specific
ornament so habitually that leaving it out is like making a wrong
note. One is the cadential trill, and another is the appoggiatura
occurring at cadences in Italianate recitative. It is in cases such as
these that ornamentation may be not only a decoration but a
necessity.

Free ornamentation

The effect of improvising variations or melodies by way of free
ornamentation is to set the performer in a peculiarly personal relationship, almost tantamount to identification, with the composer.
That is always to some extent a necessary condition for good

interpretation; but here it extends not only to the expression but to some of the notes. Even the listener must be able to share in the experience by living it through in his own person, and has something to bring to the creative partnership.

Just as Geminiani or Tartini or Leopold Mozart, when playing Corelli, did not try to sound exactly like Corelli, but rather like some compatible renewal of Corelli, and just as J. S. Bach put at least as much of himself into his very fine and free ornamentation of Vivaldi, so we within the limits of our talent may hope to draw upon our own temperamental affinity and responsiveness in order to produce free ornamentation which is at the same time alive and compatible.

(197) Diego Ortiz, Rome, 1553: 'Everybody' ornaments 'in his own style'; and if a few 'perfect consonances' [i.e. ungrammatical consecutives] occur, 'this is unimportant since at that speed they cannot be heard'.

(198) Hermann Finck, Wittenberg, 1556: 'Truly in my opinion embellishments both can and should be scattered through all the voices, but not all the time, and indeed in appropriate places, and not simultaneously in all voices . . . but so that one embellishment can be heard and picked out expressly and distinctly from another, yet with the composition whole and unharmed.'

(199) Giovanni Camillo Maffei, Naples, 1562: Ornament 'the last but one syllable of the word, so that, with the ending of the word, the ornamentation also is ended'. It is true that 'when ornamentations are being performed, many ungrammatical notes are introduced'; but 'the ornamentation by its rapidity and its delightfulness hides the faults of grammar so that neither offensiveness nor incorrectness can be experienced'.

(200) Lodovico Zacconi, Venice, 1592: 'The singer who with a little ornamentation in good time goes not too far afield will always be better appreciated than another who digresses far too much'; and in particular, 'opening passages' when fugal 'should always be set forth simply and clearly so that the entry of each part may be the better heard'.

(201) Jacopo Peri, Florence, 1600: 'Those pretty and graceful' embellishments 'which cannot be written, and writing them, cannot be learned from writing'.

(202) Giulio Caccini, Florence, 1602: [In the expressive interests of the words] I have 'placed the consonances on long syllables, and avoided short, and observed the same rules in making [ornamental] passages, although for a certain adornment I have sometimes used

some few quavers . . . over short syllables for the most part'; and although 'long windings of the voices' are perfectly acceptable 'in less impassioned music, and over long syllables, and not short, and on final cadences'.

(203) Agostino Agazzari, Siena, 1607: 'As ornamentation, we have those [improvising melodic instruments] which make playfulness and counterpointing, thereby rendering the harmony more pleasant and resounding', with 'original and diverse variations and counterpoints above the given bass'.

(204) Scipione Cerreto, Naples, 1608: 'The good and perfect player of the cornetto must have a good knowledge of the art of counterpoint, so that he can make up varied [i.e. improvised ornamental] passages at his ease'; likewise a trumpeter must 'know how to make up counterpoint'.

(205) Bartolomeo Barbarino, Venice, 1614: 'The vocal part' is written out 'in two ways, simple and ornamented. The simple for those who do not have the disposition [for ornamental elaboration], and for those who have counterpoint and the disposition, who will be able by themselves to make up ornamental passages'; but 'the ornamented, then, for those who, having the disposition, do not have counterpoint to be able to make up variations, as properly one must'.

(206) Enrico Radesca, Venice, 1617: The compositions as written out 'are not given ornamental passages, in that those who by nature are not endowed with the disposition may not at all be deprived of the work'; indeed, and 'however skilful the singer may be, he will never extemporaneously perform that ornamental passage exactly as it is written down'.

(207) [Vincenzo Giustiniani, about 1628]: 'Articulate the words well in such a manner that one may hear even the last syllable of each word, which should not be interrupted or overlaid by passages [i.e. improvised variations] or other ornaments.'

(208) Giovanni Battista Doni, [Rome, about 1635]: Ornamentation can be most elaborate 'in Theatres [i.e. opera]; in Churches, where above all one should use grave and moderate singing', long ornamentations 'are extremely unsuitable. In chambers, similarly, where one usually sings some sort of refined melody, and in the company of people who understand Music, it is necessary to use them not so much as one says abundantly, but more sparingly.'

(209) Pietro della Valle, [Rome], 1640: 'Playing in the company of other instruments does not require the artifices of counterpoint so

much as the graces of art; for if the player is good, he does not have
to insist so much upon making a display of his own art as upon
accommodating himself to all the others', taking turns 'to sport with
gracefulness of imitations'; for good players 'will show their art in
knowing how to repeat well and promptly what another has done
before; and in then giving room to the others and fit opportunity for
them to repeat what they have done'; but 'in the company of voices',
still more restraint is needed, and 'to support a chorus', nothing
beyond 'good chords and pretty accompaniments, which should
follow the voices gracefully'. [Very relevant when we are realizing
the missing orchestral elements in early Italian operas.]

(210) Bénigne de Bacilly, Paris, 1668: 'A piece of music can be
beautiful and please not, for want of being performed with the
necessary embellishments, of which embellishments the most part
are not marked at all on paper, whether because in fact they cannot
be marked for lack of signs for that purpose, or whether it has been
considered that too many marks encumber and take away the clearness of a melody, and would bring a kind of confusion; besides, it is
useless to mark things, if you do not know how to fashion them with
the necessary adaptations, which makes all the difficulty.' Moderation is desirable throughout, while 'everyone agrees that the less one
can make ornamentations in the first verse, the better, because they
certainly prevent the melody from being heard in its true form'.

*(211) Jean-Baptiste Lully, quoted by Le Cerf de la Viéville, Brussels,
1704–6:* 'No embellishment! My recitative is only for speaking, I
want it to be absolutely plain' [though in the airs, as opposed to the
recitative, Lully permitted his father-in-law, Michel Lambert, to
coach his singers in some at least of the currently fashionable free
ornamentation, besides the many smaller ornaments which even
from his recitative were not totally excluded].

(212) Roger North [early eighteenth century]: 'It is the hardest task
that can be to Pen the Manner of artificial [i.e. with art] gracing an
upper part; It hath been attempted and in print, but with Woefull
Effect.' [North thus criticized the Amsterdam edition, promptly
pirated in London, of Corelli's Opus v with ornamental versions for
the slow movements 'composed by Mr A. Corelli as he plays them',
a claim never substantiated and virtually disproved by their becoming, after a fair start (possibly a genuine recollection) in No. 1,
woeful indeed; so that North was moved to ask] 'how so much
vermin could creep into the works of such a master'. North con-
cluded that 'the spirit of that art is Incommunicable by wrighting,
therefore it is almost Inexcusable to attempt it'. [A pardonable
exaggeration, perhaps, but still an exaggeration.]

(213) Johann Adolf Scheibe, Hamburg, 1737: J. S. Bach, by writing out his ornamental passages in notation, 'not only deprives his pieces of beauty and harmony but makes the melodic line utterly unclear' [unfortunately worded, and from a different standpoint; but compare Bacilly at *(210)* above].

(214) J. A. Birnbaum in reply to the above, Leipzig, 1738: Free ornamentation 'is bound to distress the ear markedly and to destroy the fundamental melody if the performer introduces it at the wrong moment', or unsuitably; if all performers 'knew how to introduce it where it may function as a genuine embellishment and special emphasizing of the fundamental melody, then there would be no point in the composer writing down in notes what they knew already'; but since the majority do not know, J. S. Bach or any other composer 'has the right' to notate such ornamental passages 'in accordance with his desires'.

(215) [John Hawkins, ?London, about 1740]: Agostino Steffani 'would never admit of any [ornamental] divisions, or graces, even on the most plain and simple passages, except what he wrote himself' [almost certainly an exaggeration, like the similar claims by Gluck a generation later; but indicative all the same].

(216) Pier Francesco Tosi, Bologna, 1723, in English, London, 1742: 'In the first section [of a da capo aria] they require nothing but the simplest Ornaments, of a good Taste and few, that the Composition may remain simple, plain and pure; in the second they expect, that to this Purity some artful Graces be added, by which the Judicious may hear, that the Ability of the Singer is greater; and in repeating the *Air* [i.e. in the da capo repeat of the first section], he that does not vary it for the better, is no great Master'. Nevertheless: 'Seek for what is easy and natural.'

[Of cadenzas]: 'Every *Air* has (at least) three *Cadences,* that are all three final. Generally speaking, the Study of the Singers of the present Times consists in terminating the *Cadence* of the first Part with an overflowing of *Passages* and *Divisions* at Pleasure, and the *Orchestre* waits; in that of the second the Dose is increased, and the *Orchestre* grows tired; but on the last *Cadence,* the Throat is set a going, like a Weather-cock in a Whirlwind, and the *Orchestre* yawns' [satiric, of course, but as such a timely warning; indeed, many arias need at most one brief cadenza leading back to the da capo recapitulation].

(217) Joachim Quantz, Berlin, 1752: Ornamental passages must [*a*] be such that 'the main notes, on which the ornamentations are made, shall not be overshadowed'. They are chiefly for adagio, since [*b*] 'the plain melody ought in allegro as in adagio to be ornamental and

made more pleasing by appoggiaturas, and other small essential
ornaments', but [c] 'the allegro does not admit many free ornamentations'. However, [d] it is merely bad taste 'to load the adagio
with a quantity of ornamentation, and to disguise it in such a way
that often among ten notes there is scarcely one which is in harmony
with the fundamental part, and the principal melody of the piece can
hardly be heard any longer'. [e] 'For the pieces in the French style
are mostly pieces characterized and composed with appoggiaturas
and trills, in such a way that hardly anything can be added to
what the composer has written; whereas in music composed in the
Italian style, a great deal is left to the wishes and capacity of the
performer.'

[f] In a trio sonata 'the ornamentation ought to be such that it
not only suits the subject, but can also be imitated by the second
part', i.e. 'in passages which consist in imitations'; for 'if the two parts
have the same melody one against the other, in sixths or in thirds,
nothing [freely ornamental] should be added, unless it has been
agreed beforehand to make the same ornamentations'. [g] In a
quartet 'there is still less liberty'; [h] in a concerto the soloist should
not ornament freely if 'the accompanying parts make tuneful melodies', but 'if they are only the plain harmony', then 'all kinds of
ornamentation can be made [by the soloist], provided the rules of
harmony, taste and reason are not violated'.

[i] A cadenza is 'that spontaneous ornamentation which is made
by a solo part, at the close of a piece, over the last note but one of the
bass part, namely over the fifth of the key in which the piece stands,
according to the free will and pleasure of the performer', in order [j]
'to surprise the hearer unexpectedly once more at the end, and in
addition to leave a particular impression on his feeling', though [k]
'cadenzas must flow from the principal feeling of the piece', and [l]
'for a singing part or a wind instrument must be so constituted that
they can be made in one breath. A string player can make them as
long as he likes, in so far as he is otherwise rich in invention. Yet he
achieves more advantage through a reasonable shortness than
through a tiresome length'.

(218) James Grassineau, London, 1740: 'Canto Fioretti [literally,
flowery song] is a song full of diminutions, graces, passages, *etc.*,
and is indeed figurate counterpoint.'

(219) Jean-Jacques Rousseau, Paris, 1768: 'Passage' means 'composed of many notes or divisions which are sung or played very
lightly'. [The most important of all practical recommendations
whether for the composer's or the performer's figurations.]

Suggestions for free ornamentation

Since no two modern performers are going to approach their free ornamentation with quite the same gifts or quite the same tacit assumptions, it would be an impertinence to draw up rules; but the following suggestions may perhaps be confirmed from the evidence sampled above and the music examples below:

(i) Ornamenting the parts of vocal polyphony requires of the performers mutual tact and restraint *(198, 200)*, the first entries particularly being left quite or almost plain.

(ii) In the reciting style now commonly known as monody, ornamental passages are an enhancement, but must show the greatest consideration for the words – always the primary concern in the reciting style. Long syllables rather than short should carry them *(202)*; the final syllable of the phrase should be left plain *(199, 207)*; the note before the last is a particularly good point for an extensive ornamentation; impassioned passages should be sung more simply and expressively than unimpassioned passages *(202)*.

The pioneers of the reciting style were virtuoso singers, like Caccini and Peri, who favoured vocal display in appropriate passages. Their music contains many striking examples in writing, and others were improvised in performance according to the singer's taste. Thus Caccini's *Nuove Musiche,* published at Florence in 1602, includes an aria (but so free that it is almost arioso) from his opera *Il Rapimento di Cefalo*, as 'sung, with the ornamentation shown', by the celebrated bass, Palantrotti, quite floridly but only on words especially inviting it, like *suave*, sweet, *mortale*, mortal, *ale*, wings, *risvegliario Amore*, awaken Love; then a tenor aria is printed with similar ornamentation, but this is reported as having been sung in the actual performances 'with different ornamentation, according to his own style, by Jacopo Peri'.

(iii) The improvisation of elaborate ornamental parts by melodic instruments of the early baroque orchestra was subject to similar considerations to those described for voices, including not getting in each other's way; not getting too showy or too contrapuntally ambitious; ornamenting especially on the last note but one, and not at all on the last note; ornamenting more for opera than for church or chamber; and in general aiming rather at expressive embellishment than at personal display *(203, 204, 207, 208, 209)*.

It is an undecided question how far this strange art of improvising a whole orchestral texture above a given bass spread (Praetorius *(220)* certainly introduced it into his German volume of 1619), or how long it lasted; but it may have accounted for the frequent appearance in the scores of early baroque operas of instructions for orchestral interludes and accompaniments with no music written out, or only a bass pedal note, or a bass line, or a bass line with empty staves left open above it for upper melodies never filled in, but presumably worked out in rehearsal more or less on the spur of the moment. For modern performance, we may have to write it out.

The Italian reciting style was known in France from Caccini's visit of 1605 onwards; and still better known after De Nyert's visit to Rome in 1638. From these and other contacts, a flourishing national style of bel canto composing and singing developed in France, though not until Lully a national style of opera. The two main leaders of French bel canto were Bénigny de Bacilly, who called his important treatise *(221) Sur l'art de bien chanter* in literal translation of the Italian term; and Michel Lambert, whose influence grew still wider when Lully married his daughter in 1664, and he became (or remained) a regular coach to Lully's singers. The ornamentation of French airs by the singers thus trained persisted throughout the seventeenth century and beyond: predominantly free; but including many partially defined specific ornaments *(222)*. Another strain of ornamentation began with the French lutanists of the seventeenth century, from whom it passed to the great harpsichordists such as François Couperin, his predecessors and his successors; it also spread to Germany, including J. S. Bach. The gambists such as Marais and the flautists such as Hotteterre drew upon both these strains, but perhaps most upon the vocal strain. By the beginning of the eighteenth century, many specific ornaments had taken somewhat stricter shape, while free ornamentation was radically reduced in quantity by comparison with the Italian styles.

(iv) For free ornamentation in French music of the seventeenth century, especially for the voice and for such favoured melodic instruments as the gamba and the flute, the scope was wide *(210)*. When Lully evolved a genuinely French style of recitative, more lyrical and melodious than Italian recitative was by then becoming, he precluded from it the free ornamentation which he admitted in the airs; and even the smaller ornaments should be introduced very sparingly *(211)*.

The Italian bel canto was meanwhile evolving the da capo aria under several categories such as melancholy, brilliant, furious and the like, each needing its own appropriate style of ornamentation. Cadenzas were customary (more especially at the end of the middle section); and the recapitulation of the first section – the da capo repeat – was meant to be relieved from undue obviousness by the judicious invention of improvised variations: 'such new and ingenious embellishments as, in Italy, every singer of abilities would be expected to produce each night it was performed', Dr Burney *(223)* explained.

(v) For the first section of da capo arias, little if any free ornamentation is required, and few specific ornaments; for the middle section, not much more; for the da capo repeat, considerably more, yet not so as to distort or obliterate the original melody *(215, 216)*: cadenzas, if introduced, should be of moderate proportions.

Similarly with the composing, more or less by improvisation, of an actual melody for that common class of adagio which Dr Burney *(224)* called 'little more than an outline left to the performers abilities to colour'. With whatever proportions of preparation, memorization or improvisation, this melody must sound as if it were being made up by spontaneous invention *(213, 214, 218, 219)*. Structural notes (i.e. those written) may generally be performed more strongly than the flexible chains of ornamental notes connecting them. Sometimes, however, an accented passing note may take the beat, thus postponing and lightening a structural note. Unaccented passing notes whether few or many, arpeggiation whether simple or partially melodic, and changing notes in every variety are further resources.

(vi) The musical material used for creating an ornamental melody out of a mere structural skeleton as notated should have that relevance and consistency which all good composition demands *(212, 213, 214, 217)*; the effect in performance being kept light in emphasis and unfettered in rhythm *(218, 219)*.

Examples of free ornamentation

Ex. 73. Giulio Caccini, opening of 'Ardi, cor mio', (a) as notated plain in Florence, Bibl. Naz., MS Magl. xix.66, p. 131 (and almost identically in Brussels, Bibl. du Cons., MS 704, pp. 77–8; (b) as notated ornamentally in Caccini's *Nuove Musiche*, Florence, 1602 (collated by H. Wiley Hitchcock and reproduced here by kind permission):

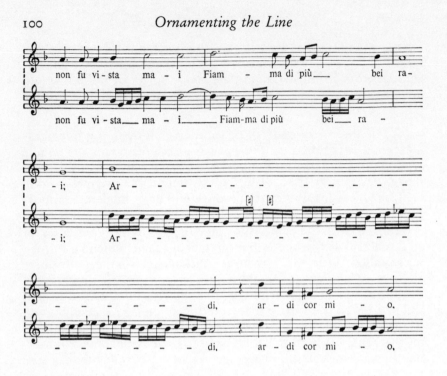

Ex. 74 (by kind permission of Vincent Duckles):

"Care-charming Sleep"   1. from Ms Don. c. 57
(Robert Johnson)   2. from Ms Fitzwilliam 52. D. 15
                               3. from BM Ms Add. 11,608

Ex. 75. M. de la Barre, *Airs à deux parties*, Paris, 1669, pp. 12ff., slight additional ornamentation at 2nd couplet of vocal sarabande:

Ex. 76. George Frideric Handel, cantata 'Dolce pur d'amor l'affanno', early 18th century, facsimile of autograph in Cambridge, Fitzwilliam Museum, MS 30–H–2, by kind permission of the Syndics; ornamentation of voice part, and inconsistent notation of rhythms all meant as dotted, (a) p. 10, end of aria; (b) p. 12, the same in another key, with similar but not identical notation of ornamentation:

(a)

(b)

Ex. 77. Geminiano Giacomelli, *Merope*, Venice, 1734, opening of 'Quell' usignolo', (a) as written; (b) as sung with free ornamentation, including a relatively brief cadenza, by Farinelli (properly Carlo Broschi), repr. by Franz Haböck, *Die Gesangskunst der Kastraten*, Vienna, 1923, p. 140, from an unspecified manuscript in Vienna (actually Österreichische Nationalbibliothek MS 19111 No. 3):

Ex. 78. Corelli, Op. v, No. 1, (a) in first ed., (b) ornamentation from Roger's ed. of ?1715 (perhaps after Corelli here, at a fairly long remove):

Ex. 79. Arcangelo Corelli, Violin Sonatas, Op. v, Rome, 1700, No. 9, with free ornamental elaborations (first half of 18th century) by Francesco Geminiani, printed by Sir John Hawkins, *A General History . . . of Music*, London, 1776, ed. of 1875, II, pp. 904ff. (and in Hans-Peter Schmitz, *Die Kunst der Verzierung*, Kassel, 1955, 2nd ed., Kassel, 1965, pp. 62–9); play the appoggiaturas short, accented, on the beat:

Giga Allegro

Adagio

[tr]

Last movement; versions collated by Sol Babitz and privately communicated:

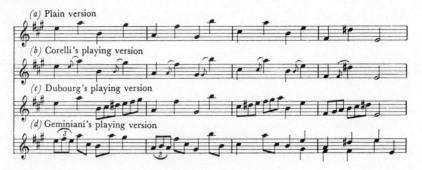

(a) Plain version

(b) Corelli's playing version

(c) Dubourg's playing version

(d) Geminiani's playing version

Ex. 80. J.-B. Loeillet, Sonata in F major for flute, violin or oboe, Largo, last bars, brief written out cadenza (ed. Hinnenthal, Berlin, 1945):

Ex. 81. Corelli, Op. v No. 7, (a) as notated; (b) my sample ornamentation; (c) for repeat:

Sarabanda; largo

[*not too slow*]

Chapter Eight · Specific Ornaments

An open situation

The ornamentation of long passages, however free, tends to run to formulas which can be taught orally. From the sixteenth century these were also taught by many text-books which systematized the oral tradition, so that, for instance, Coclico *(225)* recorded in 1552 that 'this is the first ornamentation which Josquin taught his own pupils'. Thence in turn emerged shorter segments which, together with other effects apparently suggested by the natural idioms of the voice and various instruments, can be regarded as specific ornaments.

At no stage was there any final distinction between free ornamentation and specific ornaments. The names, the signs and the behaviour of ornaments crossed and multiplied so inconsistently that any classification is liable to be somewhat arbitrary. This is especially true in the early development of specific ornaments. Later in the baroque period a certain amount of standardization occurred, chiefly as a result of what may be called the appoggiatura principle.

Whether insinuated ornamentally, or integrated later in history into the composed structure, it is the principle of the appoggiatura to accent on the beat (with or without preparation) a dissonance resolved after the beat on to the postponed main note, so that the harmony is changed and intensified. The effects on melody and rhythm are still important considerations; and indeed, consonant appoggiaturas can actually weaken the harmony, and in consequence are not much lingered upon. But it was the harmonic consequences of the accented dissonant appoggiatura which became so significant for the course of music, and which helped to impose on certain specific ornaments a more obligatory behaviour than they had previously displayed.

(226) Jean Rousseau, Paris, 1687: 'You must practise all the ornaments in all their fullness, especially the prepared [appoggiatura-like] trill and the appoggiatura.' [Nevertheless] 'Avoid a profusion of ornamental figures, which only confuse the melody and obscure its beauty'.

(227) Michel de Saint-Lambert, Paris, 1707: 'It would only be taking a slight licence for one part to make even a perfect fifth twice in succession with another part. I know the greatest strictness would not have it; but since this fault (if it is one) does not show at all, I hold that one can make it unhesitatingly', and that 'since music is made only for the ear, a fault which does not offend it is not a fault'. [Opinions differed and continue to differ as to what constitutes in practice an offence to the ear; but for the principle, compare *(197)* and *(199)* above, and Ex. 92 below.]

'Good taste is the only rule'; though 'there are ornaments which are necessary', of which 'the most important is the trill', for the rest 'you may ignore all that I have shown' and 'make new ones in accordance with your taste' [the customary opinion, to which Couperin at *(228)* below affords a less typical but none the less interesting contrast].

(228) François Couperin, Paris, 1722: 'I am always surprised (after the pains I gave myself to mark the ornaments which suit my Pieces, of which I have given, incidently, a clear enough explanation [if only it were!] in my special Treatise, known under the title of The Art of Playing the Harpsichord) to hear of people who treat them without respecting them. This is an unpardonable neglect, in view of the fact that it is not at all an optional matter to take such ornaments as one wishes. I declare then that my pieces must be performed as I have marked them.' [Compare *(197)* above; not in fact the accepted opinion, as the need to protest by implication confirms; but much nearer to being so in France than elsewhere.]

(229) J. A. Scheibe, Leipzig, 1745: 'The conductor must see to it that all the violins use the same ornaments as their leader.'

(230) Joachim Quantz, Berlin, 1752: 'It is true that the ornaments of which we have spoken are absolutely necessary for good expression. All the same they must be used in moderation'; while 'in passages which resemble one another, the variations ought not always to be the same'. [But contrast C. P. E. Bach at *(231)* below, requiring consistency in imitations.]

(231) C. P. E. Bach, Berlin, 1753: [a] 'In justice to the French it should be said that they mark their ornaments with scrupulous exactness. So too do the masters of the harpsichord in Germany, yet without carrying their ornaments to excess.' But [b] 'since our present taste, to which the Italian bel canto has contributed so much, requires other ornaments in addition to the French, I have had to draw on the ornaments of various countries. I have added some new ones to these. I believe that the best style of performance, on whatever instrument, is the one which skilfully unites the accuracy

and brilliance of the French ornaments with the smoothness of Italian singing'; however, [c] 'the ear can accept more movement from the harpsichord than from other instruments'; while [d] 'the expression of simplicity or of sadness admits of fewer ornaments than other feelings'; and [e] it is always best to avoid confusion caused by 'ornaments of many notes', and 'many ornaments on rapid notes'. For [f] 'above all, the extravagant use of ornaments is to be avoided'.

[g] 'All imitations [in contrapuntal textures including fugues] must be exact down to the last detail. Hence the left hand must practise ornaments until it can imitate them efficiently.' However, [h] 'the notes of an ornament adapt themselves to the sharps and flats of the key signature', with certain expressive exceptions or necessary modifications 'which the trained ear at once recognizes' [and the trained player supplies].

[i] 'All ornaments shown in little notes belong to the following note. Thus while the previous note is never curtailed, the following note loses as much of its duration as the little notes take away from it'; that is to say [j] 'the little notes rather than the following main note are sounded with the bass and the other parts. One slinks through them right into the following note; it would on the contrary very often be a mistake to fall in a rough manner on to the main note'. [Ed. of 1787 adds] 'It might be thought unnecessary to repeat that the remaining parts including the bass must be sounded with the first note of the ornament. But as often as this rule is invoked, so often is it broken.' [This protest implies that the practice defended was not so uniform as the author desired.]

(232) F. W. Marpurg, Berlin, 1756: 'Regarding the smaller ornaments, they are so essential at most places that without their strict observance no composition can please the more refined ears.' [1765]: 'But where does one learn what notes are given ornaments or at which point of the melody this or that ornament ought to be introduced?' [Marpurg might have added: and with what nuance of execution?] 'One should hear persons who are reputed to play elegantly, and one should hear them in pieces one already knows. In this way one may form one's taste, and do likewise. For it is impossible to devise rules to meet all possible cases, so long as music remains an inexhaustible ocean of options, and one man differs from the next in his response.'

Wise words indeed. Among so many points upon which rules give way to taste, we may notice Saint-Lambert *(227)*, like Ortiz *(197)* and Maffei *(199)*, defending in practice theoretically ungrammatical progressions if the ear accepts them, as J. S. Bach and other good contrapuntalists must have agreed since such progressions do óccur (hardly by mistake and not very probably by inadvertence) in their written music. It is not, however, necessarily to be regarded as an ungrammatical progression, though it is certainly a bold one, when the second of two consecutive perfect fifths is an accented passing note to a note of resolution which the mind takes for the point of arrival: this met, for example, with Telemann's approval as a particularly strong and justifiable treatment for the long appoggiatura shown at Ex. 92 below.

C. P. E. Bach's insistence at *(231)* that all specific ornaments in cue-sized notes (whether notated before or after a bar-line) necessarily take the beat is borne out by others of that flourishing Berlin school, such as Marpurg, but is in more general terms a serious overstatement. We might better put it that ornaments whose behaviour falls under the appoggiatura principle necessarily take the beat, including the long appoggiatura itself, the appoggiatura-like species of cadential trill, and sometimes, but not always, the slide, the mordent and the turn.

The appoggiatura

The term comes from the Italian *appoggiare*, to lean, and implies an auxiliary note, usually dissonant, always stressed, on the beat, and slurred to its declining resolution on the main note. The auxiliary may be from above or from below: by step diatonically, at the tone or semitone according to the prevailing tonality (unless chromatically modified for expressive effect); or by leap (standard only in recitative, by the drop of a fourth). The length varied from moderate in the early baroque, to a choice between decidedly long or decidedly short in the late baroque. The shorter the appoggiatura, the more brilliant and the less significant for the harmony; the longer, the more expressive and the more significant for the harmony. A very slight silence of articulation before the appoggiatura may enhance its brilliance or its expressiveness as the case may be.

When either the long or the short appoggiatura will fit the harmony, the choice rests with the performer, since the notation if any is very seldom intended to be literally indicative of length. In late baroque music, with the partial exception of the French, there is a general presumption in favour of the long appoggiatura, with its characteristic intensification of the harmonic progression; if, however, the effect is to confuse or to weaken the harmony, a short appoggiatura may be desirable instead.

Ex. 82. J. Playford, *Introduction*, London, 1654 (eds. 1660 on), appoggiaturas:

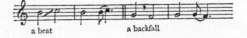

a beat   a backfall

Ex. 83. Appoggiaturas in H. Purcell's posthumous *Lessons*, London, 1696:

a forefall   a backfall

This appoggiatura of moderate length did not disappear from later baroque music, and in some contexts it is the obvious solution, as either melodic or more probably harmonic considerations will suggest. But from the last years of the seventeenth century onwards we meet evidence to suggest that the standard appoggiatura now took half the length of an undotted main note; two-thirds of the length of a dotted main-note; all the first of two tied notes in compound triple time; and all of a note before a rest.

Ex. 84. D'Anglebert, *Pièces de Clavecin*, Paris, 1689, appoggiaturas (cheute ou port de voix):

Ex. 85. J. M. Hotteterre, *Principes*, Paris, 1707, p. 28, appoggiaturas at (a) probably, at (b) probably not, on the beat:

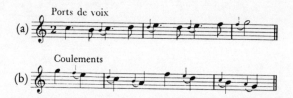

Ports de voix

(a)

Coulements

(b)

The length of the cue-sized notes at (b) is misleading as so often.

Ex. 86. Dieupart, *Suites de Clavecin*, Paris, c.1720, appoggiaturas:

Port de voix   Cheute
Forefall up   Backfall

Ex. 87. J. S. Bach, *Clavier-Büchlein*, begun Cöthen, 1720:

Accent   Accent
steigend   fallend

Ex. 88. Johann Mattheson, *Vollkommene Capellmeister*, Hamburg, 1739, II, iii, 24 and 25, appoggiaturas by leap:

(233) *Joachim Quantz, Berlin, 1752:* 'Hold the appoggiatura half the length of the main note'; but if dotted 'that note is divided into three parts, of which the appoggiatura takes two, and the main note one only: that is to say the length of the dot.' Of two notes tied in compound triple time, 'the appoggiatura should be held for the length of the first note including its dot'; an appoggiatura before a rest 'is given the length of the note, and the note the length of the rest'.

Ex. 89. Joachim Quantz, *Essay*, Berlin, 1752, end of book, Table VI, Figs. 11, 13, 15, 17, 23 to be performed as Figs. 12, 14, 16, 18, 24:

Appoggiaturas may sometimes be taken at more than normal length for reasons of expression.

(234) *Francesco Geminiani, London, 1751:* The expressive appoggiatura 'should be made pretty long, giving it more than half the length or time of the Note it belongs to'; the short appoggiatura lacks that expressive quality, 'but will always have a pleasing effect, and it may be added to any note you will'.

(235) *J. E. Galliard, London, 1742:* 'You dwell longer' on the appoggiatura than on the main note.

(236) *C. P. E. Bach, Berlin, 1753:* 'The general rule for the length of the appoggiatura is to take from the following note, if equal [duple],

half its length; and if unequal [triple], two-thirds of its length'; but sometimes it 'must be prolonged beyond its normal length for the sake of the expressive feeling conveyed. Sometimes the length is determined by the harmony.'

(237) *F. W. Marpurg, Berlin, 1765:* 'One must no more introduce faulty progressions with an appoggiatura than one may count on an appoggiatura to save consecutive fifths.' [Contrast *197, 199, 227;* but the very fact of being a long appoggiatura means that any faultiness will not be covered up by speed, though with a short appoggiatura it may be.]

In Ex. 90 below, the first pair of appoggiaturas would normally occupy a crotchet's length, pushing the main notes forward into the following rest; but this makes impossible harmony on the third beat. The second pair, having no following rest, will by rule and by necessity alike be quavers, at normal length. Later (mm. 44–5) the same effect is written out at quaver length. The obvious solution is therefore quaver length throughout.

Ex. 90. J. S. Bach, Prelude XVIII from Book II of the 'Forty-Eight', appoggiaturas:

In Ex. 91 below, the normal length for the appoggiatura in the second bar is a quaver, giving, to the eye, consecutive fifths between beat one and beat two. But this is nevertheless correct, since the C natural sounds to the ear like an accented passing note to the B natural, and this is an acceptable and indeed an excellent progression, as Ex. 92 confirms, where the same progression is presented as desirable.

Ex. 91. François Couperin, *Pièces de Clavecin*, Livre I, Paris, 1713, Cinquième Ordre, mm. 9–10, (a) as notated, (b) as the appoggiatura may best be interpreted:

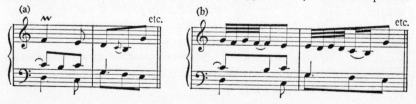

Ex. 92. Georg Philipp Telemann, *Musikalisches Lob Gottes*, Nürnberg, 1744; acceptable consecutive fifths shown with approval at (a); this can be written out as at (b); which is heard as if it were the grammatically correct progression at (c).

(238) Joachim Quantz, Berlin, 1752: Short appoggiaturas 'take their value from the notes before which they stand'; they 'are performed very briefly', but likewise 'on the beat of the main note'.

(239) François Couperin, Paris, 1716: Appoggiaturas are struck 'with the harmony, that is to say in the time which would be given to the following [i.e. main] note'.

(240) J. E. Galliard, London, 1742: 'You lean on' the appoggiatura 'to arrive at the [main] note intended'.

(241) F. W. Marpurg, Berlin, 1765: 'All appoggiaturas . . . must come exactly on the beat' together with 'the accompanying parts . . . only the main note to which the appoggiatura is the auxiliary being delayed'; the appoggiatura 'should always sound a little louder than the main or essential note, and should be gently slurred on to it'.

(242) C. P. E. Bach, Berlin, 1753: 'All appoggiaturas are performed more loudly than the following note', and 'are joined with it, whether slurs are written or not'.

(243) Joachim Quantz, Berlin, 1752: 'It is a general rule that one should make a small separation between the appoggiatura and the note which precedes it, above all if the two notes are at the same pitch; so that one can make the appoggiatura distinctly heard.' Appoggiaturas 'can make a great contribution' to the harmony; 'for they become dissonances, as fourths and sevenths', which 'are resolved by the following [i.e. main] note'. Thus 'it is not enough to know how to perform the appoggiaturas according to their nature and difference, when they are marked; it is also necessary to know how to put them in suitably when they are not written'.

(244) C. P. E. Bach, Berlin, 1753: 'Appoggiaturas are among the most necessary ornaments. They enrich the harmony as well as the melody. . . . Appoggiaturas change chords which in their absence would be too straightforward. All syncopations and dissonances can be attributed to them. Where would the art of harmony be without these ingredients?'

Ex. 93. C. P. E. Bach, *Essay*, Berlin, 1753, illustrations for 11, ii, 8:

It will be realized that in the above examples the cue-sized notes represent the appoggiaturas which C. P. E. Bach suggests should be put in by the performer.

Ex. 94. C. P. E. Bach, *Essay*, Berlin, 1753, 11, ii, 11. strange effect on the rhythm caused by long appoggiatura normally prolonged:

Ex. 95. Leopold Mozart, *Violinschule*, Augsburg, 1756, ix, 4, showing the growing tendency to very long appoggiaturas:

C. P. E. Bach *(245)* also suggests certain contexts in which the short appoggiatura (which has no appreciable effect upon the harmony) may be appropriate: e.g. 'before quick notes' or 'before long notes when a note is repeated' or 'with syncopation' or 'when the appoggiaturas fill in leaps of a third'. [But C. P. E. Bach does not here exclude long appoggiaturas, of which he gives many instances in such a situation.] 'But in Adagio the feeling is more expressive if they are taken as the first quavers of triplets and not a semiquaver'; while the appoggiaturas 'before [notated] triplets are taken short so as to avoid obscuring the rhythm'; and 'when the appoggiatura forms an octave with the bass it is taken short [because of the weak harmony it would make if long enough to affect the progression]. If a note rises a second and at once returns . . . a short appoggiatura may well occur on the middle note.'

Ex. 96. C. P. E. Bach, illustrations (there are others) to the above:

Appoggiaturas in recitative

In mid-baroque and subsequent Italian or Italianate recitative, appoggiaturas are required on two cadential formulas. One formula is the drop of a fourth, prepared before the beat, which the appoggiatura takes. The appoggiatura postpones the notated main note by one half, when this main note is single (i.e. in the masculine ending, having the rhythm: 'I am a man'); and it replaces the first occurrence of the main note, when this main note is doubled (i.e. in the feminine ending, having the rhythm: 'I am a woman'). (See Ex. 98 below.) The other formula is the drop of a third, which the appoggiatura fills in, unprepared, on the beat, likewise postponing the main note in a masculine ending or replacing the first occurrence of the redoubled main note in a feminine ending. (See Ex. 99 below.) The musical rhythm although not the poetical rhythm is the same in all these cases: the appoggiatura takes the accent, and half the duration.

There do not seem to be any basic exceptions to these conventions. The addition of the ornament is not optional, but an obligatory correction of misnotation recognized by every trained musician. In a masculine ending it was *possible* to ignore the convention so as to produce a deliberate effect of dramatic directness, and the modern performer may also take this liberty on occasion, provided he is aware of what he is doing. It is important, however, for singers and conductors today to recognize the regular necessity for such appoggiaturas in recitative. This necessity exists for any period at which Italianate recitative remained an active tradition. It is of paramount importance, for example, in the recitatives of Mozart.

An early and amusing proof of this convention comes in a satirical Italian cantata, anonymous, but found in a manuscript of the middle of the seventeenth century, when the later variety of Italian recitative (less melodious and more stylized than the earlier variety) was just beginning to emerge, and with it, evidently, the conventional manner of half-singing, half-declaiming it to which these cadential appoggiaturas belong. The word *accenti* shown at (a) in Ex. 97

below means appoggiaturas; its music crosses exactly that gap of a descending third which a duly accented appoggiatura on the beat is intended to fill in; the joke is that the notation does not introduce it but the singer does – or there would be no joke; my recommended interpretation is given at (e). We may likewise assume an improvised swelling and decreasing on *messe di voce* and a true unmeasured trill on *trilli*; there is a short notated passage (or tirata) on *passaggio*, no doubt open to further extension in performance. At (b), (c) and (d) there are feminine endings in the words which at least invite cadential appoggiaturas either from above or from below (compare Ex. 98 and Ex. 99).

Ex. 97. Anonymous, 'Se voi vi credete sentirmi cantare', *c.*1650–70, Paris, Bibl. Nat., MS Vm⁷. 2, f. 10v, satire on ornamentation:

Ex. 98. G. P. Telemann, *Cantatas*, Leipzig, 1725, preface, masculine and feminine endings both shown as requiring appoggiaturas in recitative:

(246) Johann Mattheson, Hamburg, 1739: 'The customary method of notation [two C's on a six-four harmony, is for purposes of illustration here written F dropping to C], as it would be sung.'

(247) J. A. Scheibe, Berlin, 1757: 'The notation of the feminine cadence with the dropping fourth . . . differently from what is sung . . . is undoubtedly regrettable, because in the nature of things we should not write differently from what is sung, and because many uninstructed singers can be led astray by this, especially in the middle of a recitative.'

Ex. 99. J. A. Scheibe in F. W. Marpurg's *Kritische-Briefe*, Berlin, for 1760–2, letter 109, p. 352, thus illustrated:

(248) J. F. Agricola, Berlin, 1757: It is a matter of course that 'one sings' for cadences dropping a fourth 'the next to last note a fourth higher' than it is notated.

The double appoggiatura

There is an ornament sometimes called the double appoggiatura, which encloses its main note from below and above with two auxiliaries, mostly by steps adjacent to the main note, but sometimes starting by leap. On the beat, this may lean and be slurred somewhat like an ordinary appoggiatura; before the beat, it is slurred but does not lean, merely consisting of a pair of disjunct, unaccented changing notes.

The passing appoggiatura

There is also an ornament sometimes called the passing appoggiatura, much favoured in France, and in Germany under French influence towards the end of the baroque period. It falls between beats, and when slurred to the previous beat it is a conjunct unaccented passing note such as occurs readily enough in free ornamentation; but when slightly emphasized and slurred to the following beat, it is a specific ornament, perhaps belonging to the emerging rococo rather than to the traditional baroque.

(249) Joachim Quantz, Berlin, 1752: 'There are two sorts of appoggiaturas. One is taken, like accented notes, on the down beat; the other like [unaccented] passing notes, on the up beat of the bar. The first could be called striking, and the other passing appoggiaturas.' In 'the French style of performing, from which these [passing] appoggiaturas are derived' the slurs go across the beat and 'one must hold the dots long and stress the notes on which the slurs start'.

Ex. 100. Joachim Quantz, *Essay*, Berlin, 1752, illustrations for VIII, 5, passing appoggiaturas:

The less mannered alternative of slurring across the beat but without emphasizing the passing appoggiatura was recommended by Leopold Mozart, and may well have been the more normal (because more natural) method of performance.

(250) Leopold Mozart, Augsburg, 1756: 'Passing appoggiaturas [unlike standard appoggiaturas] do not belong to the time of the main note on to which they fall but must be taken from the time of the note before'; thus 'the semiquaver is taken quite smoothly and quietly, the accent always coming on the quaver'.

Ex. 101. Leopold Mozart, *Violinschule*, 1756, IX, 17, passing appoggiaturas:

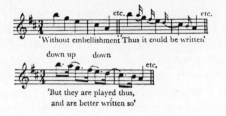

'Without embellishment 'Thus it could be written'

down up   down

'But they are played thus,
and are better written so'

Marpurg and the Berlin school in which C. P. E. Bach was prominent so disliked any ornament before the beat that we read:

(251) F. W. Marpurg, Berlin, 1755: 'All appoggiaturas . . . must fall exactly on the beat.'

Ex. 102. F. W. Marpurg, *Anleitung*, Berlin, 1765, Tab. III, passing appoggiaturas disapproved:

(a) written   (b) [wrong]   (c) [wrong]   (d) [right]

The normal manner of performing passing appoggiaturas in French and French-influenced music is shown, fortunately without rhythmic ambiguity, in Ex. 103 and Ex. 104 below. The notation gives the ornament as taken before the beat and slurred to it. There is nothing to indicate the between-beat stress as recommended by Quantz at *(249)* above; the more natural accentuation on the beat, as described by Leopold Mozart at *(250)* above, is therefore a reasonable presumption unless otherwise preferred.

Ex. 103. Étienne Loulié, *Elements*, Paris, 1696, *port de voix* (i.e. passing appoggiatura):

Ex. 104. Jean-Jacques Rousseau, *Dictionnaire de musique*, Paris, 1768, Plate B, passing appoggiatura:

written

performed

Signs for the passing appoggiatura, if notated, are often indistinguishable from signs for the ordinary appoggiaturas, whether long or short. These choices may therefore be made at the performer's option, provided that any influence on the harmony is duly considered. In later baroque music an ordinary long appoggiatura best meets the majority of contexts and is best supported by the evidence in contemporary text-books: except that when an appoggiatura, as occasionally happens, turns a dissonant main note into a consonance, it becomes rather weak to linger on it, and short or fairly short will as a rule sound more satisfactory. But indeed it will be appreciated that the performer's option in such matters was always meant to be quite open within the potentialities of the style, and that we are often here comparing tendencies rather than requirements. The temperamental preference of an individual performer is a perfectly valid factor in the equation. Ornaments between beats are smoother and less influential upon the harmony; ornaments on the beat are stronger and more influential upon the harmony. With appoggiaturas as with some other ornaments, our choice within the appropriate possibilities may quite properly be conditioned by our individual dispositions.

The slide and the tirata

The slide is a short section, and the tirata is a longer section of a diatonic (or sometimes a chromatic) scale, ascending or (less often) descending. Both of these are very ordinary occurrences in free ornamentation; but the slide in particular acquired some distinctness as a specific ornament. It takes two forms of equal validity though different effect: as an ornament before the beat, to which it then leads up with a certain grace and elegance; and as an ornament on the beat, to which it thereby lends added force and prominence, although the effect upon the harmony, if any, is likely to be much milder than the effect of an ordinary long appoggiatura. Personal preference may again, within limits, quite properly condition the choice of behaviour where the notation or the harmony does not; but the evidence from notation is perhaps more frequently suggestive here.

On keyboard instruments the first note of the slide, if consonant, may optionally be held on while the third note strikes, the second note being dissonant and released so soon as sounded: an effect identical with the passing acciaccatura to be described below. The rhythm of the slide may either be equal, or (especially at slow tempo) dotted; the expression may either be robust (especially at quick tempo) or lingering. My own preference, other circumstances permitting, is for a fairly fast and well-accented slide taken firmly on the beat, even in slow or moderate tempos. In quick tempo, I may take the slide somewhat faster but still on the beat, which gives a

very brilliant and incisive crispness to the rhythm. Under all circumstances, the slide is slurred forward to its ensuing main note.

Ex. 105. John Playford, *Introduction*, London, 1654 (eds. from 1660 on), descending and ascending slides:

Ex. 106. Jacques Champion de Chambonnières, *Pièces de clavecin*, Paris, 1670, on
the beat slide:

Ex. 107. Jean Henri D'Anglebert, *Pièces de clavecin*, Paris, 1689, on the beat slides:

Ex. 108. J. G. Walther, 'Praecepta', 1708, slides anticipating the beat:

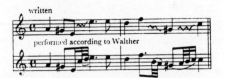

Ex. 109. J. S. Bach, 'Trauer-Ode 1', *Neue-Bach-Ausgabe*, I, 38, pp. 181–203, m. 18,
unison passage for oboe d'amore 1 (with slide written out in ordinary notation)
and soprano voice (with the same slide notated by a sign), showing slide taken in
the regular manner on the beat (inequality is presumed in the voice to match the
dotted notation in the unison oboe d'amore):

Ex. 110. C. P. E. Bach, *Essay*, Berlin, 1753, II, vii, very extended slide:

Ex. 111. ibid., normal slides:

Ex. 112. F. W. Marpurg, *Clavier zu spielen*, Berlin, 1750, slides in various rhythms:

The acciaccatura

Two baroque forms of the acciaccatura were recognized: (a) the simultaneous acciaccatura, a dissonant auxiliary struck with the main note on its beat but rapidly released; (b) the passing acciaccatura, a dissonant auxiliary struck between two main notes (most commonly a third but sometimes a fourth apart) and released while they are still sounding.

The simultaneous acciaccatura is a forceful ornament for the keyboard. Francesco Geminiani *(252)* described it in 1749 as 'perform'd by touching the key lightly, and quitting it with such a spring as if it was Fire'; C. P. E. Bach *(253)* in 1753 wrote that 'of the two notes struck together, only the upper one is held, the lower one being at once released'.

The passing acciaccatura is also an ornament for the keyboard, where it can add to the sonority a shimmer of transient dissonance particularly valuable for accompaniment, above all in recitative. It helps to build up interesting, though not unduly defined, sonorous support; and it makes the requisite arpeggiation more ringing and more diversified, yet with none of the distraction which melodic figuration would introduce undesirably in such a context. Passing acciaccaturas can be multiplied in the same chord, which may thus become what Geminiani *(254)* in 1749 called 'dissonant with respect to the fundamental Laws of Harmony; yet when disposed in their proper place [they] produce that very Effect which it might be expected they would destroy'.

Vincenzo Manfredini *(255)* in 1775 still confirmed that 'These Acciaccature make a better effect when the Chords are executed in Arpeggio form, as one is accustomed to when accompanying Recitatives.' However, they also have a valuable place in solo music for the harpsichord. Their notation, when shown at all, was various, but it was quite common to write out all the notes, main and auxiliary, at the same size, so that the chord, as so often in Domenico Scarlatti, looks like a remarkable tone-cluster. How soon, if at all, the auxiliaries are released, so that the rest of the chord goes on sounding in normal harmony, depends partly on its length and speed, partly on the boldness of the performer's disposition.

Ex. 113. C. P. E. Bach, *Essay*, Berlin, 1753, 11, v, 3, simultaneous acciaccatura:

Ex. 114. C. P. E. Bach, *Essay*, Berlin, 1753, 111, 26, 'an arpeggio with an *acciaccatura*':

Ex. 115. J. S. Bach, Partita vi, Sarabande, passing acciaccaturas, (a) as written; (b) as it might alternatively have been written; (c) approximately as performed:

The trill

The trill is a more or less rapid alternation of a main note with an upper auxiliary one degree (i.e. a tone or a semitone) above.

No ornament has had a more varied or interesting history; but much of its complication disappears when it is understood that the trill has not one main function to perform, but two. One is melodic and rhythmic decoration and coloration; the other is harmonic modification and intensification. Both were current throughout the baroque period; but during the second half of it, the harmonic function assumed prominence to such an extent that its behaviour in practice influenced the behaviour of the melodic function, as was shown by a very rare consensus indeed among textbook descriptions, tables of ornaments and documentary evidence of this kind, in favour of an upper-note start.

The trill can be seen emerging among the many written-out specimens of free ornamentation before and early in the baroque period. Though already tending to merge into uncounted repercussions rather than to retain the regularity with which they may commonly be seen notated, these trill-like figures often kept both the melodic interest and the inventive variety of their sources; and even when the specific ornament which we describe as the trill took firmer shape, it still showed the traces of its origins in the more wayward tradition of free ornamentation. Its behaviour remained flexible whenever its chief purpose was melodic decoration. In particular, its manner of starting varied between the upper note and the lower note, with consequent varieties of accentuation and to some extent of placing. In this melodic and decorative capacity, the trill is a specific but nevertheless a fluid ornament, and no dependable rules can be set up for its interpretation.

But with the development of the typical cadential formulas of the baroque period, the trill increasingly attached itself to those formulas, until by about half way through the period it became virtually impossible to arrive at an authentic cadence (plagal cadences do not afford the same invitation) without introducing a written or an unwritten trill or trills. These can best be distinguished as cadential trills, and they follow standards of behaviour far more regular than can be defined for trills in general. Cadential trills have mainly a harmonic function, which they fulfil by behaving like appoggiaturas, accented from the upper (i.e. the auxiliary) note, on the beat, so that the harmony is heard from that upper note, to which the main note then serves like a resolution. Even when decorative prefixes, and occasionally suffixes, are grafted on to the body of such a cadential trill, this appoggiatura-like harmonic functioning may remain intact. The resulting melodic enhancement may then provide a sort of outer wrapping, but the intensification of the harmonic progression is still the main consequence. A harmonic trill is an upper-note trill, and if this upper note causes a relaxing rather than an intensifying of the harmony, a harmonic trill is not appropriate. Cadential trills are necessarily harmonic trills, that being their prime reason for existence. Other trills may (and frequently did) borrow the behaviour of cadential trills – but from option and habit rather than from necessity.

By far the majority of baroque cadences neither require nor tolerate any decorative appendages to their cadential trills. The slight flicker of melodic interest and the marked increase of harmonic interest are exactly what the situation requires, and it is only necessary to slip in the standard cadential trill firmly but unostentatiously, treating it as nothing so very special, but simply as an ordinary matter of course. In effect, a cadence notated as dominant 5–3 to tonic 5–3 may then become (according to the trill or trills employed) dominant 5–4 or 6–3 or 6–4 resolving (as the main note catches the attention) through dominant 5–3 to tonic 5–3: a perfectly straightforward but rather more eventful progression which somehow makes all the difference. The taste for cadences (like the taste for sequences), and with them the obligation to bring in their implied cadential trills, was so ingrained in baroque musicianship that it is equally useless to play them down or to play them up: they must just be taken philosophically with a proper nonchalance. For those who do not like cadences, sequences and cadential trills, baroque music is not the scene.

(256) Fray Tomás de Santa María, Valladolid, 1565: 'Take care not to make the redoble [a trill-like formula] too long with the effect of making the music clumsy.' [The implication is that the measured notes are not necessarily confined to a literal count.]

(257) Girolamo Diruta, Venice, title-page 1609 (actually 1610): 'The tremolo [here meaning a trill-like formula], if played lightly and gracefully and appropriately, makes the music live and sound beautiful', alternating not 'with the note below' [i.e. as a mordent-like formula], but 'with the note above'. (See Ex. 120.)

(258) Girolamo Frescobaldi, Rome, 1615–16: 'You must not divide the trill note for note, but only make it rapid.'

(259) J. A. Herbst, Nuremberg, 1642: 'You beat as many' repercussions 'in the trill as you desire'.

(260) Anon. English, after 1659: 'Prepare all long shakes [trills] .... The Note before a Close is to be Shaked .... All shakes are taken from the note above.'

(261) Bénigne de Bacilly, Paris, 1668: The trill is 'one of the most important ornaments, without which the melody is very imperfect'. Its termination 'is a join made between the trill and the note on which it is desired to arrive, by means of another note touched very

delicately'; for 'although the composer has not marked on paper the joins after the trills . . . it is a general rule to assume them, and never to suppress them, otherwise the trill will be maimed, and will not be complete'. [This is an important point.]

(262) Jean Rousseau, Paris, 1678: [a] 'There are two sorts of trill; that is to say the trill with leaning (*avec appuy*), and the trill without leaning (*sans appuy*).' [2nd ed. of 1683; 1st ed. of 1678 has 'support' (*support*): an alternative and very convenient, though less literal, translation for *appuy* is 'preparation'; Cotgrave's *Dictionarie (263)*, London, 1611, has for *support* 'a prop or stay' and for *appuy* 'a stay, buttresse, prop, rest, a thing to leane upon', so that the meaning here is the appoggiatura-like leaning when the upper-note start is prolonged.]

'The trill with leaning is made when the finger which has to shake the trill, leans (*appuye*) for a little, before it shakes, on the note which is immediately above the one which requires a trill.' [Cotgrave has for *appuyer* 'to rest, or lean on'; Quantz *(264)* in his French edition of 1752 uses *appuyer* as the equivalent for his German phrase 'to bring length (*Länge*)', thus confirming that leaning implies and includes prolonging.]

[b] 'With regard to notes on the same degree, the leaning should be very slight, at least if it does not fall on a final cadence, and with regard to other notes that should be leaned upon, it is always necessary to regulate the leaning according to the value of the note, and according to the measure and the movement, which ought never to be altered, under any pretext of ornamentation.' In particular, [c] 'the last note but one of every final cadence, when descending by step, requires the trill with leaning'. And on the other hand, [d] 'the trill without leaning is made like the foregoing, while lessening the leaning *(en retrenchant l'appuy)*' [i.e. reducing the length of the appoggiatura-like upper-note start, though not omitting it: Cotgrave gives under *retrancher* 'diminish, lessen, abridge'. It seems therefore that this passage does not refer to trills starting on the main note, though such trills did occur. Here, 'without preparation' means prolonging the upper-note start less, and 'with preparation' means prolonging the upper-note start more – i.e. with less or more of an appoggiatura-like effect. This is confirmed by *266, 268, 271* and *277* below, and evidently refers not to universal but to fairly standard practice.]

(265) Le Sieur Danoville, Paris, 1687: 'If there is a trill marked on the Mi, you anticipate (*anticiper*) on the Fa [i.e. a semitone above], putting the first finger on the Mi, and the second on the Fa, which is the auxiliary (*supposeé*) note, and holding the first leaned upon (*appuyé*) you let the bow slur (*couler*) for a moment, then you agitate

the second finger with an equal agitation [i.e. the upper note anticipates the main note (though *not* the beat, to which no reference is
made); and such leaning by the auxiliary, so that the main note is
pushed forward to begin a little after the beat, is recommended as
normal for] perfect, imperfect, middle and final cadences in all the
modes'. [Notice that '*couler*' above implies behaving like an appoggiatura, one French term for which was *coulé*.]

(266) Étienne Loulié, Paris, 1696: 'The trill is an appoggiatura
(*Coulé*) repeated two or more times from a little sound (*petit son*)
[i.e. auxiliary note] to an ordinary [i.e. notated main] note, one
degree lower. . . . When the voice lingers appreciably (*demeure
sensiblement*) on the little sound of the first appoggiatura, this is
called preparing [or "leaning upon"] the trill (*appuyer le
tremblement*). . . . The preparation of the trill should be longer or
shorter in proportion to the duration of the note trilled.' After being
thus prepared 'the trill should begin within the beat on which the
trilled note begins. . . . When the voice does not linger appreciably
on the first note [consisting] of the first appoggiatura, the trill is
called unprepared trill (*non appuyé*), or without preparation (*sans
Appuy*). The appoggiatura of the trill ought not to be jerked
(*secoüez*) . . . but slurred (*licez*) [*sic: ?liez*] as much as possible as if
there were only one sound'. Make trills 'quicker or slower, in
proportion to the quickness or slowness of the piece'.

(267) Sébastien de Brossard, Paris, 1703: 'One should beat very
quickly in alternation, or one after another, the two sounds on
conjunct degrees . . . one starts with the higher, and one finishes
with the lower.'

(268) Jacques Martin Hotteterre, Paris, 1707: Trills begin 'on the
sound above', and are slurred; the preparation may extend up to
'about half the duration of the note, especially in grave movements',
while 'the number of repercussions is governed solely by the length
of the note. . . . It is necessary to point out that the trills or shakes
are not always marked in musical pieces' [a masterly understate-
ment]. Also Paris, 1737: 'The trill is always prepared from its upper
Note (*se prépare toujours de sa Note superieure*).'

(269) François Couperin, Paris, 1713: 'It is the length of the note
which should decide . . . the greater or lesser numer of strokes, or
repercussions.' [1716/17]: 'Although the trills are marked as regular
in the table of ornaments in my first book [of 1713], they are
nevertheless to begin more slowly than they finish.' [This does of
course depend very much on the context, and Quantz' advice to trill
at a constant speed, cited at *(274)* below, is more widely applicable.]

(270) T[homas] B[rown], London, 1704, 3rd and only surviving ed., 1722: 'Always let the Proper [main] Note be distinctly hear'd at the last'.

(271) Pier Francesco Tosi, Bologna, 1723: [a] 'Whoever has a very fine trill, even though he were short on (*scarso di*) every other ornament, always enjoys the advantage of bringing himself without offence to the cadences, where it is generally most essential. . . . [b] The trill for its fineness (*per sua bellezza*) wants to be prepared (*preparato*); nevertheless, its preparation (*preparazione*) is not always required (*non sempre esige*), since neither time (*Tempo*) nor taste (*gusto*) will always permit it [although] it is called for in all final cadences.' As in *(262)* and *(266)* above, 'preparation' means here the appoggiatura-like prolonging of the upper note start which even when shortened is still assumed to be present. Tosi included no musical examples, but this meaning is confirmed by those quite correctly added by J. E. Galliard *(272)* in his English translation of 1742 (having, as he says, heard Tosi and wishing to make his teaching 'more universally known, when a false Taste in Musick is so prevailing'); and also, independently, by Johann Friedrich Agricola *(273)* in his German translation and expansion of 1757 (perhaps retaining the influence of J. S. Bach with whom he studied). By *bellezza*, Tosi probably referred to that long-enduring tradition of Italian bel canto to which his book and its translations so authentically contributed. [For a more general confirmation that singers in the first half of the eighteenth century were taking an appoggiatura-like upper-note start to the cadential trill as a matter of course, see G. P. Telemann's statement to that effect in a footnote to Ex. 5, m. 8 of his *Generalbass-Übingen*, Hamburg, 1733–5, quoted below with my Ex. 164, where he writes that 'of course' the singer will take the (unnotated) 4 'before the trill comes'. This expectation was indeed the normal one by that time in such situations, whether vocal or instrumental, and no ambiguity should arise in contexts of that variety.]

(274) Joachim Quantz, Berlin, 1752: [a] 'Trills give great brilliance to performance, and just like appoggiaturas are indispensable. . . . [b] There is no need to make all trills with the same speed'; for example, 'in sad pieces the trills are made slowly; but in gay pieces they ought to be made more quickly', though in either direction [c] 'you must not fall into any excess'. [d] Trills are, however, best made 'at a constant or similar speed, and one kept to a moderate rapidity. . . . [e] Each trill starts . . . with the appoggiatura' [i.e. the appoggiatura-like upper note], [f] 'often as quick as the other notes which form the trill', but 'whether long or short' it should be given a fresh attack, whereas 'the trill and its termination ought to be

slurred'; and [g] this termination 'consists of two little notes, which follow the note of the trill and are made at the same speed'. When not written into the notation, 'both the appoggiatura and the termination must be understood'.

(275) C. P. E. Bach, Berlin, 1753: [a] The appoggiatura 'is found before cadential trills'; [b] 'trills on notes of a certain length are played with a termination' taken [c] 'as quickly as the trill itself'.

(276) Leopold Mozart, Augsburg, 1756: In course of a passage 'not only is an appoggiatura made before the trill, but the appoggiatura is held through half the duration of the note, while the trill is not started till the remaining half. But if a passage begins with a trill an appoggiatura [though still present] is hardly heard, and in such a case is nothing but a strong attack on the trill'. And 'the slow [trill] is used in sad and slow pieces; the medium in pieces which have a lively but yet a moderate and restrained tempo; the rapid in pieces which are very rapid and full of spirit and movement; and finally the accelerating trill is used mostly in cadenzas and with gradual crescendo'; yet 'the trill must above all else not be played too rapidly'.

(277) F. W. Marpurg, Berlin, 1756: 'A trill, wherever it may stand, must start with its auxiliary note.' Even 'if the upper note with which a trill should begin immediately precedes the note to be trilled, it has either to be renewed by an ordinary attack, or has, before one starts trilling, to be connected, without a new attack, by means of a tie, to the previous note'. [This is an important clarification; and still more important is the following from the French edition, also Berlin, 1756:] 'The leant-upon (*appuyé*) or prepared (*préparé*) trill' is 'when one lingers a little time on the auxiliary note before making the repercussion, or when one starts with a slow repercussion and increases the speed by a kind of gradation'.

The following relates to the baroque trill in its various uses:

(i) Because the melodic and the harmonic functions of the baroque trill overlap, and because the trill can occur in so many different contexts, the variations in its performance were evidently numerous then, and are hard to trace now with any certainty. But in effect, the freer variants are those which serve the melody and may be pursued to individual taste; the more formal conventions are those which serve the harmony, and are subject to the appoggiatura-like behaviour which actually produces their harmonic consequences.

(ii) In its harmonic function, the trill begins on the beat with its upper (auxiliary) note. This initial upper note is necessarily accented, and optionally prolonged to emphasize its appoggiatura-like effect. The stress is heard to fall on the auxiliary, of which the main note therefore sounds like the resolution. Thus a cadence notated merely as dominant 5-3 to tonic 5-3 may (according to the trill or trills introduced) be heard as dominant 5-4 (or 6-3, or 6-4) resolving through dominant 5-3 to tonic 5-3 (see Ex. 140 below). It is this audible diversion of the harmony (occasionally made visible in the continuo figuring) which, together with the energy imparted by the repercussions, can enliven those otherwise somewhat un-eventful dominant to tonic cadences so characteristic of later bar-oque music. Rather than trying to play these cadences down, it is important to endorse them unostentatiously but confidently with the cadential trills which they imply whether so marked or not. The function of such a cadential trill is not merely decorative, but affects the progression in an almost obligatory particular.

(iii) When there are prefixes and occasionally suffixes attached to the trill, these may be decorative yet not supplant the harmonic functioning of the trill; or they may be structural and take their own share in this harmonic functioning. (See Ex. 152 and Ex. 153.)

(iv) In its melodic function, the trill carries no such appoggiatura-like obligation. A trill which is not intended for harmonic function-ing can as well start from its lower note, if the melody is thought to lie better that way. This occurred most freely during the first half of the baroque period. During the second half, there appeared very numerous tables of ornaments, and these are very consistent in showing the accented upper-note start, either in the body of the example, or more rarely (Ex. 129 and Ex. 130) as a written-out preparation giving the same instruction yet more emphatically. Whether necessary or not, therefore, the upper-note start seems by the middle of the baroque period to have become habitual, though not invariable. And so it continued far into the nineteenth century.

(v) Subject to the above qualifications, we may describe a standard baroque trill. It takes the beat; it has an upper-note start, necessarily accented and optionally prolonged; and it sounds both strong and natural in a very wide variety of contexts. But to produce this intended effect, it requires great certainty in its handling. If its upper-note start comes half-heartedly, and still more if it comes unaccented just before the beat, instead of accented right on the beat, the balance is turned upside down, so that we hear the trill as a main-note trill with a note of anticipation and not as an upper-note trill with an appoggiatura-like emphasis: quite a different effect and most disappointing if it happens inadvertently. The characteristic feature of a standard baroque trill is its intensification of the harmony. The accentuation from the upper note and the resolution on to the main note are what produce this intensification.

(vi) The accenting and prolonging of the upper-note start may be minimal, in which case the trill may be described as unprepared (though it is not literally so); or maximal, in which case the trill may be described as (extensively) prepared; or of any intermediate degree.

(vii) The preparation made by the upper-note start may actually be written as a separate note, in which case it may either be briefly repeated, or tied over into the trill itself. More often it is not written, but is nevertheless to be understood. Compound preparations may sometimes be used, for which see Compound ornaments below.

(viii) The repercussions of the trill vary in number and in speed according to the context, but in the standard pattern there continues throughout a sense of their being accented from the upper rather than from the lower note.

(ix) Trills (other than half-trills and continuous trills, for which see below) must be terminated, in one of two standard ways, occasionally varied by compound terminations. The standard terminations are (a) the turned ending, normally joined to the repercussions of the trill without interruption or change of speed; and (b) the little note of anticipation, either joined to the trill by a slur, or separated from it by a silence of articulation. When written at all, these terminations may be shown in misleading rhythms. When not written, the choice is conditioned by the context. Whether written or not, one or other termination is to be understood.

(x) Except for the silence of articulation optional before a note of anticipation in the second standard termination as described at (b) under (ix) above, trills are slurred entire, whether so marked or not. (The notes of a trill bowed out separately, if used at all, are not a trill, but a fragment of free ornamentation, perhaps never intended and certainly never authenticated as a specific ornament – an unbroken flow of notes being of the essence of any real trill.)

(xi) Half-trills are seldom extensively prepared and are not terminated, consisting as they do of not more, or not many more, than two repercussions (four notes), and ending firmly on the main note. Above a certain speed, the first of these four notes tends to disappear, thus turning the half-trill *(Pralltriller)* into an even shorter inverted mordent *(Schneller)*. At any speed, the half-trill should take the beat. It is usually but not always quite quick.

(xii) Continuous trills on long notes are not so much melodic or harmonic ornaments as means of colouring or sustaining the tone.

They start on the beat, ordinarily though not necessarily on the upper note, which can be but does not need to be more or less accented or prolonged. Their speed is likely to be fairly constant; they do not require a termination, but may be well suited by a turned ending (especially if they end just before rather than just on the main beat of the bar).

(xiii) Trills on a continued series of short notes are taken on the beat, brilliantly but without need for termination, being in effect half-trills occupying almost the whole of the brief main notes on which they stand.

Examples illustrating the trill

Ex. 116. Sylvestro di Ganassi, *Fontegara*, Venice, 1535, specimen divisions showing the notes of trills:

Ex. 117. Diego Ortiz, *Trattado*, Rome, 1553, division showing notes of a trill [slur understood; see f. 3r, 'without a fresh stroke of the bow']:

Ex. 118. Giovanni Luca Conforti, *Breve et facile maniera d'essercitarsi a far passaggi*, Rome, 1593, written-out trill:

Groppo di sopra

Ex. 119. Giulio Caccini, *Euridice*, 1600, divisions ending (a) with written-out trill; (b) with implied trill (called by Caccini *groppo*):

Ex. 120. Girolamo Diruta, *Il Transilvano*, II, Venice, 1610, accelerating trill:

The intention in the above example is evidently a gradually accelerating trill, as it also is in the following.

Ex. 121. Claudio Monteverdi, *Orfeo,* 1607, Act III, accelerating trill:

Ex. 122. Biagio Marini, 'Sonata per l'organo e Violino ò Cornetto', in his *Sonate, Symphonie, Canzoni . . .* Op. 8, Venice, 1629, trill written out in measured notes but probably intended to be taken in the ordinary way with unmeasured repercussion, as is perhaps confirmed in this case by the indication *groppo* (trill):

Ex. 123. Playford, *Introduction*, London, 1654 (1660 on), table of ornaments, trill:

A Backfall
shaked

The above trill is unprepared unless the preceding crotchet G is tied to it, in which case it is prepared, the crotchet G constituting the preparation (a very common method of performance).

Ex. 124. Jean Rousseau, *Traité de la viole,* Paris, 1687, pp. 99–100, *double cadence;* (a) as notated by Rousseau; (b) as explained by Rousseau; (c) previous measure as explained by me, where Rousseau does not complete his explanation:

(a)

(b)

(c)   etc.

Ex. 125. D'Anglebert, *Pièces de Clavecin,* Paris, 1689:

Tremblement   Tremblement
simple   appuyé

Ex. 126. Purcell (or his ed.), posthumous *Lessons,* London, 1696, unprepared and prepared trills:

Ex. 127. August Kühnel, *Sonate ô Partite ad una ô due Viole da gamba, con il basso continuo,* Cassel, 1698, No. 1, m. 14, simultaneous trills in consecutive seconds (just play them boldly):

Ex. 128. François Couperin, *Pièces de clavecin,* Paris, 1713, trills (my interpretations):

(e)

Tremblement détaché

(Interpretation.)

Ex. 129. Jean-Philippe Rameau, *Pièces de clavecin*, Paris [1724], Table of Ornaments, unprepared trill, prepared trill and trill with turned ending (*double cadence*):

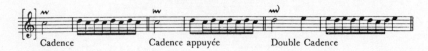

Cadence   Cadence appuyée   Double Cadence

'The note slurred (*liée*) to that which carries a Trill or a Mordent, serves as a beginning to each of these ornaments.'

Exemple   Expression [Rameau's]

Ex. 130. Vincenzo Manfredini, *Regole armoniche*, Venice, 1775, p. 27, upper-note start to a trill, likewise notated separately:

[sic]

[sic - - - - -]

Ex. 131. C. P. E. Bach, *Essay*, Berlin, 1753, II, ii, 9, upper auxiliary of trill notated here (though not ordinarily notated) in order to show the necessity for starting the trill with it even if the note before is at the same pitch; (a) my approximate interpretation according to the first alternative given by Marpurg at *(277)* above; (b) my approximate interpretation according to the second alternative given by Marpurg at *(277)* above:

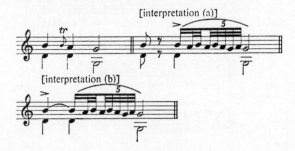

[interpretation (a)]

[interpretation (b)]

Ex. 132. (a) C. P. E. Bach, *Essay*, Berlin, 1753, II, iii, 30, 'the half or bouncing trill *(halbe oder Prall-Triller)*', as shown in his Table IV, Figure XLV; (b) context turning *Pralltriller* into *Schneller* ('jerky one') at speed, Table IV, Figure XLVIII; (c) i.e. to be interpreted, if at speed; (d) to be interpreted, if not at speed:

Ex. 133. George Frideric Handel, Sonata in C major for Viola da Gamba and Harpsichord (Handel's own realization), (a) 1st mov., m. 2, trill shown in harp-sichord by appoggiatura sign; (b) m. 4, matching trill in gamba shown by trill sign; (c) end, trills in tenths between harpsichord and gamba, notated differently but intended identically:

Ex. 134. J. S. Bach, *St Matthew Passion*, 'Erbarme dich', appoggiatura sign prob-ably indicating trill:

Ex. 135. Leopold Mozart, *Violinschule*, Augsburg, 1756, x, 6, trill terminated with note of anticipation:

Ex. 136. Henri-Louis Choquel, *La musique rendue sensible par la méchanique*, Paris, 1759, 2nd ed. 1762, p. 166, prepared trill, (a) as notated by Choquel; (b) as illogically illustrated by Choquel; (c) as I would approximately interpret it on Choquel's written instruction:

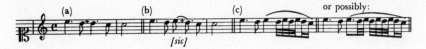

Ex. 137. J.-J. Rousseau, *Dict.*, Paris, 1768, Plate B, trill with very long preparation (his interpretation followed by mine):

Ex. 138. (a) Note of anticipation not indicated; (b) note of anticipation misleadingly indicated; (c) approximate detached interpretation; (d) approximate slurred interpretation (my examples):

Ex. 139. (a) Turned ending not indicated; (b) turned ending misleadingly indicated, but strongly implying a trill; (c) turned ending approximately indicated, and still more strongly implying a trill; (d) interpretation in all these cases (my examples):

Ex. 140. (a) Cadence notated as plain dominant 5-3 to tonic 5-3; (b) trill shown introducing dominant 5-4; (c) trill shown introducing dominant 6-3; (d) trills shown introducing dominant 6-4 (my examples):

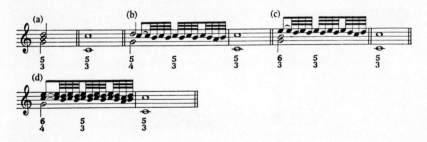

The mordent

The mordent is an alternation of a main note with an auxiliary note one degree below: the mirror opposite of the trill, and like the trill a derivative of free ornamentation (see Ex. 141 and Ex. 142 below). But whereas the trill has most importance when it is of some length and some harmonic consequence, the mordent has most importance when it is quite short (corresponding in effect to a half-trill rather than to a full trill); and starting as it does on its main note, not its auxiliary note, it has no harmonic consequence. The mordent can enhance the melody and sharpen the rhythm and even colour the harmonic texture by introducing a slightly inharmonic element; but the mordent cannot alter the progression of the harmony after the manner of a harmonic and especially a cadential trill. The chief purpose of the mordent is its rhythmic function.

The inverted mordent, alternating with an upper auxiliary, occurs in free ornamentation (see Ex. 141 below), but did not become a specific ornament of standard application in baroque music, except when a descending half-trill is curtailed to an inverted mordent under pressure of speed (see Ex. 132 above). After the baroque period, the inverted or upper mordent became a standard and indeed a fashionable ornament; but the standard baroque mordent is a lower mordent, and except at speed it should not ordinarily be replaced by an upper mordent.

Just as an appoggiatura 'leans' upon the beat, so the mordent 'bites' upon the beat, as their names imply. In both these ornaments, therefore, the standard performance is not before but on the beat, and so we find the mordent depicted in tables of ornaments where they are sufficiently unambiguous to decide the point. Couperin's table of ornaments of 1713, as at Ex. 143 (a) and (b) below, is not unambiguous in this respect; but he wrote (278) unambiguously in 1716/17 that 'every mordent must be set on the note on which it stands' and that 'the repercussions and the note on which one stops must all be included within the time-value of the main note'. This confirms, I think, that the cue-sized notes in this important table are not meant to anticipate but to take the beat, and this is also my interpretation of them elsewhere in the table (as at Ex. 128 above). A mordent anticipating the beat of the main note is not so much unauthentic as uncharacteristic: as with the slide, the effect is smoother, and the mordent under most circumstances is not smooth but crisp.

(279) *Le Sieur de Machy, Paris, 1685:* To make a mordent [on the viol], 'lift the finger from the note as soon as sounded, and replace it at the same time' [a perfectly comprehensible illogicality].

(280) Jean Rousseau, Paris, 1687: [To make a mordent, also on the viol] 'the finger stopping a note first makes two or three little repercussions more brilliantly and rapidly than a trill, and then remains on the fret. . . . The mordent is ordinarily made on the second note of an ascending semitone'.

(281) George Muffat, Augsburg, 1690: 'A mordent' is made with 'the lower auxiliary note, which is often (if the ear does not forbid it) a whole tone below'.

(282) Johann Mattheson, Hamburg, 1739: For mordents, 'first, the written main note must be sounded; then the tone or semitone below (according to the key) must be touched upon, and left for the main note with such speed that these three notes make one sound which, as it were, hesitates a little, is delayed by something, gently collides with something'.

(283) C. P. E. Bach, Berlin, 1753: [a] 'The mordent is particularly effective in an ascent by step or by leap. It appears seldom in a descent by leap, and never on descending steps of a second': [b] just 'the opposite of the half-trill', which may be used on a step 'only in descent, which is exactly where a mordent is unsuitable' [try this in reverse, and notice how weakly the ornament then anticipates the following note; also notice that an inverted mordent, on the contrary, is like a half-trill in sounding effective on a step only in descent]. [c] 'Mordents, especially short ones, lend brilliance to leaping, detached notes. [d] The mordent is of all ornaments the most freely introduced by a performer into the bass, especially on notes at the highest point of a phrase. . . . [e] With regard to accidentals this ornament adapts itself to its context in the same way as the trill. Its brilliance is frequently enhanced by raising [chromatically] its lower note.'

Ex. 141. Fray Tomás de Santa María, *Arte de tañer fantasía*, Valladolid, 1565, sect. 8, (a) inverted (upper) and (b) standard (lower) mordents ('single quiebro'):

Ex. 142. E. N. Ammerbach, *Tabulatur*, Leipzig, 1571, double mordents:

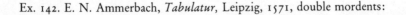

Ex. 143. François Couperin, *Pièces de clavecin*, Paris, 1713, (a) single (b) double, (c) continued mordents:

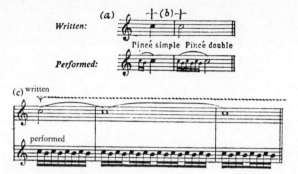

Ex. 144. Gottlieb (Theophil) Muffat, *Componimenti*, Augsburg, ?1735, semitone mordents, diatonic and chromatic:

Ex. 145. Johann Mattheson, *Vollkommene Capellmeister*, Hamburg, 1739, Pt. 11, Ch. 3, 56, chromatic mordent:

'So it is written'   'So, more or less, it is sung'.

The notation above is not mathematically logical, but the intention is clear. The semitone is here effected by an accidental sharp; but though not in the key-signature, it is diatonic to the key of G in which the example evidently stands.

Ex. 146. C. P. E. Bach, *Essay*, Berlin, 1753, 11, v, 11, (a) chromatic mordents, the D sharp shown (for demonstration only) above the mordent sign; (b) my approximate interpretation:

The turn and other changing or passing notes

These too are fragments of free ornamentation which more or less shaped up as specific ornaments.

The turn encircles its main note with a pair of upper and lower auxiliary notes, in effect changing notes: either accented on a beat, or unaccented between beats; and starting either from the upper auxiliary (standard turn), or from the lower auxiliary (inverted turn). The rhythm may vary from equal to more or less unequal. Unaccented turns, having a melodic function, are commoner than accented turns, having also a harmonic function; standard turns are commoner than inverted turns; and equal turns are commoner than unequal turns, especially if quick enough for an unequal rhythm to sound jerky. There is also a five-note turn sounding the main note before the usual four notes of a standard turn; whether accented or unaccented, it can have only a melodic and not a harmonic function.

The springer introduces an unaccented changing note between two accented main notes, with melodic but not harmonic effect; or an unaccented passing note of anticipation may be similarly introduced. The rhythm may vary between crisp and lilting, at different speeds; but the most characteristic instances are moderate and flattering.

Ex. 147. (a) J. S. Bach, *Clavier-Büchlein vor Wilhelm Friedemann Bach*, 1720, accented upper turn in equal rhythm; (b) C. P. E. Bach, *Essay*, Berlin, 1753, ed. of 1787, II, iv, 24, unaccented upper turn in unequal rhythm:

Ex. 148. (a) John Playford, *Introduction*, London, 1654, eds. 1660 on, table of ornaments, upper springer; (b) F. W. Marpurg *Anleitung*, Berlin, 1755, Table IV, upper and lower springers:

Ex. 149. Notes of anticipation, (a) John Playford, same table; (b) F. W. Marpurg, same table:

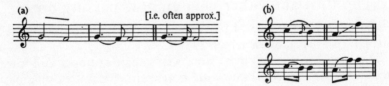

Compound ornaments

Two or more ornaments may run consecutively, producing in some cases a compound ornament. The following are among the possibilities.

(284) Jean Rousseau, Paris, 1687: 'The mordent is always inseparable from the appoggiatura, for the appoggiatura must always be terminated by a mordent' [an exaggeration which the evidence does not literally support for any time or place; but the conjunction was certainly a strong favourite with the French, and with those under French influence in Germany].

(285) J. M. Hotteterre, Paris, 1707: 'Often one links mordents with appoggiaturas.'

(286) Johann Mattheson, Hamburg, 1739: 'In singing, there is hardly an ascending appoggiatura without a mordent.'

(287) C. P. E. Bach, Berlin, 1753: 'When it follows an appoggiatura, the mordent is taken lightly, in accordance with the rule governing the performance of appoggiaturas' by which they diminish in volume on to their resolutions.

The trill was also subject to a considerable variety of prefixes, some though not most of which may alter or prevent its appoggiatura-like harmonic functioning. But when, for example, a cadential trill follows out of a more or less elaborate cadenza, or out of some briefer melodic ornamentation, what is prefixed is no part of the trill, which may still emerge intact to serve its habitual harmonic purposes. When, on the other hand, the trill forms part of a relatively specific compound ornament, its effect may well be modified without ceasing to be harmonic, as can be seen from several of the examples given below.

Ex. 150. Henry Purcell (or his ed.), *Lessons*, London, 1696, 'beat' (meaning short appoggiatura with mordent):

Ex. 151. G. T. Muffat. *Componimenti,* ?1736, appoggiaturas with and without mordents:

Ex. 152. J. S. Bach, *Clavier-Büchlein*, 1720, ascending and descending trills (two very specific compound ornaments):

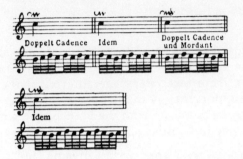

Ex. 153. F. W. Marpurg, *Principes*, 1756, Tab. v, ascending and descending trills:

Ex. 154. Christopher Simpson, *Division-Violist*, London, 1659, p. 12, double relish:

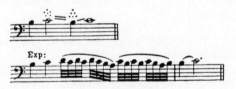

Ex. 155. L'Affilard, *Principes*, 1694, double cadence ('double cadence coupée') – (a) as written; (b) as explained; (c) as presumably intended:

Ex. 156. Georg Muffat, *Florilegium 1*, 1695, double cadence:

Other possible rhythms for this double cadence (my examples):

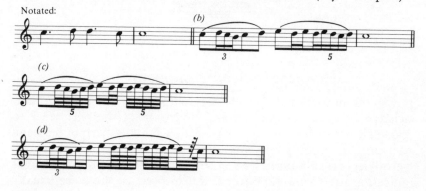

Ex. 157. J. S. Bach, (a) E major Violin Sonata, end of first movt., written out double cadence in harpsichord against ordinary cadential trill in violin; (b) D major Fugue, Bk. 1 of the 48, as the end of it might be ornamented with a particularly elaborate double cadence:

Chapter Nine · Accompaniment

Improvised composing

It was the normal and confident assumption of the baroque musicians to rely upon the tact and invention of the performer to realize, more or less by improvisation, a suitably harmonized and well-turned accompaniment above a continuo or thorough (through) bass: a figured bass in so far as it bears figures and signs indicating the harmonic outline, but in practice these are usually incomplete or lacking, and are hardly ever really dependable. Performers were habitually trained in composing too, and could mostly meet the situation as required.

(288) Lodovico Viadana, Venice, 1602: 'The organist is required to play the organ part in a straightforward manner, especially in the left hand; if he wants, however, to introduce some movement into the right hand, for example, by embellishing the cadences, or by some suitable free ornamentation, he must perform this in such a way that the singer or singers shall not be covered or confused by too much movement.'

(289) Michael Praetorius, Wolfenbüttel, 1619: 'When there are few voices singing, few keys should be touched . . . so that the voices can be heard clearly and distinctly above the organ; but when more voices begin to sing, more keys and fuller harmony should be used.'

(290) Lorenzo Penna, Bologna, 1672: 'In the ritornelli, or in the pauses intended to rest the singer, the organist must perform something of his own invention, in imitation of the Arietta or other lively matter which has just been sung. . . . Take care to arpeggiate the chords so as not to leave empty spaces on the [plucked keyboard] instrument. . . . It is always excellent to play legato, so as not to distract from the vocal part.'

(291) Matthew Locke, London, 1673: 'For the prevention of successive Fifts [sic]and Eights in the Extream Parts . . . the certainest way for the Beginner, is, to move his Hands by contraries: That is, when one Hand ascends, let the other descend.'

(292) Andreas Werckmeister, Aschersleben, 1698: 'The figures and the discords are not always written in with a view to being blindly reproduced; but a performer skilled in composition can see from them what is the composer's intention, and how to avoid conflicting with them with any matter which would be injurious to the harmony.'

(293) Friedrich Erhard Niedt, Hamburg, 1700: 'If the singer or instrumentalist sings or plays the figures which are set above the continuo, it is not necessary for the organist to play them; he can just play thirds instead if that seems suitable; or, again, it is at his own discretion if he chooses to put in something more highly elaborated.'

(294) Michel de Saint-Lambert, Paris, 1707: [a] 'The rule is, that when you have once placed the hand on the keyboard . . . you must take all the subsequent chords in the nearest possible place.' Thus [b] 'one should see if any notes of the chord one is leaving can be used in the chord which one is approaching; when that can be done, one should not change these notes'.

But [c] 'you can sometimes change the chords marked [i.e. figured] on the notes, when you judge that others will suit better'. [For example:] 'On a bass note of substantial duration, you can put in two or three different chords, although the text only asks for one'; or 'you can avoid sounding all the intervals marked in the text, when you find that the notes are too heavily laden'; or [d] 'when the measure is so compressed that the accompanist cannot conveniently play all the notes, he can content himself with playing the first note of every bar, leaving the gamba or violoncello to play all the notes'; or [e] 'if the bass has too few notes, and drags too much for the liking of the accompanist, he may add other notes by way of pleasing figuration, provided he is sure that this will not interfere with the melody'. But [f] 'do not draw so much sound from the harpsichord that it smothers the melodic part entirely, or on the contrary so little that it does not support it'.

Sometimes [g] 'one can imitate on the harpsichord the subject and the points of imitation of the song, making the parts enter one after the other. But this demands a supreme skill and it must be of the first excellence to be of any value.'

(295) Francesco Gasparini, Venice, 1708: 'One must never accompany' the melody merely 'note for note'.

(296) Lorenz Mizler, Leipzig, 1738: 'Whoever wishes to form a real conception of refinement in continuo, has only to put himself to the trouble of hearing our Capellmeister [J. S.] Bach here, who performs any continuo to a solo so that one imagines it is a concerted piece,

and as if the melody which he plays in his right hand had been composed beforehand. I can bring living witness to this, since I have heard it myself.'

(297) Johann Friedrich Daube, Leipzig, 1756: Elaborate accompaniment may be appropriate by means of 'suspensions where the composer has not written them nor shown them in the figuring'; or 'when the solo part has a rest: here one can sometimes bring in some melodic passages'; or 'in 3rds or 6ths with the solo part'; or 'when one tries to imitate the theme of the solo part, or further, at one's discretion, to let a countermelody be heard'; or if 'the bass is badly constructed', when 'the accompanist may be allowed the liberty of attempting a correction while his accompaniment proceeds'.

[Note:] 'The admirable [J. S.] Bach commanded' the elaborate style 'of accompaniment in the highest degree; when he was the accompanist, the solo was bound to shine. He gave it life, where it had none, by his abundantly skilled accompaniment. He knew how to imitate it so cunningly in either right or left hand, and again how to introduce so unexpected a counter-melody, that the hearer would ιave sworn it had all been composed in that manner with the reatest care. At the same time the regular [chordal] accompaniment was very little cut down.' This elaboration extended 'even to he bass, without interference to the solo part. Suffice it to say that whoever did not hear him missed a great deal.'

(298) Joachim Quantz, Berlin, 1752: 'The standard rule for thorough-bass is to play regularly in four parts, though for really good accompaniment it is often better not to follow this too consistently.' Another rule is that 'the hands should not move too far apart from one another, and consequently that one should not play too high with the right hand . . . it is a much better effect if the accompanying part on the keyboard is taken below the solo part, than if it is taken in unison with the top part, or actually above it' [but exceptions can of course be made].

(299) C.P.E. Bach, Berlin, 1762: [a] Where appropriate 'the accompanist may make improvised modifications in the bass line with a view to securing proper and smooth progressions of the inner parts, just as he would modify faulty figuring. And how often has this to be done!' . . . [b] 'When a bass note is figured without regard to an appoggiatura which goes with it, and this [long] appoggiatura is either compatible with the figures given, or is the same as one of them, there is no necessity, even in four parts, to modify the accompaniment. [c] But when the appoggiatura is not compatible', it 'should be played as part of the accompaniment'; or alternatively [d], one 'lets the right hand rest'. But a 'short appoggiatura' requires

no 'modification of the accompaniment'. In any circumstances, 'accompanists of experience capable and courageous enough to improvise small corrections in a piece of music should be given praise for what they do'.

[e] To effect louds and softs, 'the number of parts [in the chords] must be increased or decreased', or more or fewer chords struck 'over passing notes' in the bass. [f] 'The filled-in accompaniment' consists in 'doubling in the left hand all the notes of consonant intervals, and the consonant intervals only of dissonant chords, so far as the playing of the bass permits. This doubling must not be done low down, but close to the right hand, so that the chords of both hands adjoin, and that no space may be left between them, as otherwise the growling low notes will make a hateful confusion.' And [g] on the other hand, 'objectionable as is the accompaniment in which the upper line continuously reduplicates the melody of the main part, it is sometimes necessary, and therefore permissible, at the start of a rapid piece, particularly if this is in two parts'.

[h] 'An extended accompaniment' with notes widely spaced is sometimes rendered necessary by good voice-leading. 'Apart from such necessity, it is a familiar fact how pleasing extended harmony can sometimes be in contrast to close harmony.' [i] Elaboration in the accompaniment is particularly appropriate 'when the solo part is resting or is performing plain notes'. However, [j] 'it is sometimes a necessary and indeed a perfectly proper course for the accompanist to discuss the music with the soloist before performing it. Some prefer their accompanist to be very restrained; others the opposite.' [k] One simple and often useful recourse 'is parallel movement in thirds with the bass. The right hand is never obliged here to maintain a consistent fullness of harmony.' [l] In particular, 'transitional passages offer a challenging invitation to the inventiveness of an accompanist. But his inventiveness must be in sympathy with the feeling and substance of the music. If some reminiscence of a previous phrase can be introduced, even at the cost of slightly altering the bass part and modifying the transition, so much the better . . . so long as the solo part is not subjected to interference.' And [m] 'in short, an accompanist of judgement requires a soul full of fine musicianship, including great understanding and great good will'.

The following points are generally applicable in baroque accompaniment and can be of great importance to the effect:

(i) All appropriate textures from unisons (*tasto solo*) through two or three to four or more parts can be used and alternated, entirely according to the context. Four parts need by no means be sustained, though they are normal under many circumstances: the part-writing can be close or extended or a mixture of each. The filled-in accompaniment should not descend too low.

(ii) The realization should seldom double the melody, and not very often go above it except when accompanying solos which themselves lie low.

(iii) Imitations and counter-melodies can be most attractive where there is genuinely room for them without cluttering the texture or eclipsing the melody; such opportunities are not really very common. Imitations do not have to be exact so long as their outlines are sufficiently recognizable. Counter-melodies should nearly always be related to the composed material or drawn from it; the introduction of unrelated material, however cleverly it may be worked in, is seldom appropriate and commonly disastrous.

(iv) In many passages, perhaps a majority, a plain accompaniment serves best, enlivened chiefly by a plentiful use of accented and unaccented passing notes to keep the voice-leading melodious and the harmony interesting (accented passing notes in particular).

(v) In many other passages it is not independent counter-melodies that are needed or desirable, but simply some idiomatic figuration which brings out the most from the harpsichord without presenting any melodic rivalry to the solo parts. Enough notes can then be sounded to give the harpsichord a chance to ring, and yet there need be few heavy chords to obtrude upon the lighter qualities of the parts accompanied. Once some little figure has been thought up which serves successfully, it may be more or less carried through the movement, so as to avoid the distracting and uneconomical effect of continually bringing in fresh material. It is the relevance and the consistency of the realization which meet all ordinary needs the best.

(vi) There is no obligation to be entirely literal in reading off a continuo bass if a note changed here or a harmony altered there really works better without causing any interference to any other part. Nor is there any need to sustain a perfectly correct, and still less a perfectly even texture, for example in four regular parts where this does not suit the nature of the piece. Small faults are often acceptable; changes of texture are useful in adapting the sonority. Vitality counts for more than prudence when it comes to the performance.

(vii) It is hardly possible to make a good continuo realization without taking risks. The best is the one that best supports the music. The amount of *sonorous* support needs to be just right, neither covering up anything of significance in the solo parts, nor leaving them unsustained where they need plenty of resonance to carry them along. Furthermore, the amount of *musical* support needs to be just right as well. Too much independent interest and movement at the wrong places on the harpsichord will, it is true, distract very disadvantageously from the soloists. But on the other hand, too little going on in the harpsichord gives the sense of one partner in the team being insufficiently employed. There is an emptiness in the music where something ought to be happening. The art is to draw the material either from what is already going on in the given parts; or from some familiar storehouse of idiomatic figuration which will get the harpsichord ringing without committing it to melodic material not belonging to what is going on. When this is done with skill and insight, a continuo realization, whether it is simple or moderate or unusually ambitious, will have a wonderful way of sounding not only appropriate but also a thing complete in itself.

Accompanying recitative

Some special and rather different considerations apply in accompanying Italianate recitative. Here, everything must be sonorous and dramatic: there is no place at all for counter-melody; and no place, either, for settled rhythmic figuration. Melody hardly enters even into the solo part, which is nothing if not impulsive and declamatory; the rhythm of the soloist is quite outside the measure, being conditioned only by the words. The accompaniment must leave the solo part free, yet provide adequate support at the proper points. Show and panache may be just what is most needed here.

(300) Michel de Saint-Lambert, Paris, 1707: 'When accompanying a long recitative, it is sometimes good to dwell for a long time on one chord, when the bass allows, and to let many notes be sung by the voice without harpsichord accompaniment, then strike again a second chord, and next stop again. . . . At other times, after striking a full chord on which you dwell for a long time, you strike one note again here and there, but with such good management that it seems as if the harpsichord had done it by itself, without the consent of the accompanist. At other times again, doubling the intervals, you strike all the notes again one after another, producing from the harpsichord a crackling almost like musketry fire; but having made this agreeable display for three or four measures, you stop quite short on some big harmonious chord (that is to say, without a dissonance) as though to recover from the effort of making such a noise.'

(301) Nicolo Pasquali, Edinburgh, 1757: The art of accompanying recitative 'consists in filling up the harmony as much as possible; and therefore the left hand strikes the chords in it as well as the right.

Care must be taken not to strike abruptly, but in the harpeggio way . . . sometimes slow, other times quick, according as the words express either common, tender or passionate matters: For example; for common speech a quick harpeggio; for the tender a slow one; and, for any thing of passion, where anger, surprise, *etc.*, is expressed, little or no harpeggio, but rather dry strokes, playing with both hands almost at once. The abrupt way is also used at a punctum or full stop, where the sense is at an end.'

(302) C.P.E. Bach, Berlin, 1762: [a] 'When the declamation is rapid, the chords must be ready on the instant, particularly at pauses in the solo part where the chord precedes a subsequent entry . . . rather hurry than hold back. . . . Arpeggiation is to be avoided in rapid declamation', but finds 'its natural use' in 'slow recitative and sustained chords'. And [b] 'the slower and more expressive the recitative the slower the arpeggiation'. Also, accompanied recitatives 'in which the accompanying instruments have sustained parts are well suited by arpeggiation. But so soon as the accompaniment changes from sustained notes to short, detached notes, the accompanist must play short, firm chords, without arpeggiation, and grasped entire in both hands. . . . [c] The organ holds only the bass of recitatives accompanied by instruments with sustained parts; it takes off its chords soon after playing them . . . arpeggiation is not used on the organ. Apart from arpeggiation, the other keyboard instruments bring in no ornamentation or elaborations when accompanying recitatives. . . . [d] When completing the arpeggiation of a preparatory chord it is as well to reach the top of the arpeggio with the note on which the singer is to begin.'

Two opposite conventions affect the timing of the accompaniment at cadences in Italianate recitative:

(i) The retarded accompaniment *delays* the pair of dominant to tonic bass-notes until *after* the voice has finished, regardless of whether these are misnotated under the voice, or more correctly after the voice (and even so, needing a little extra delay to avoid hurry). And this is the standard convention in every circumstance other than opera.

(ii) The telescoped accompaniment *advances* the pair of dominant to tonic bass-notes so that the dominant comes *under* the voice, also regardless of the notation. The appoggiatura (see p. 116) may then be treated, irregularly, as an independent harmony-note (the four of a dominant six-four) which the main note has next to resolve a fourth below as the five of a dominant five-three, smartly followed by the tonic chord on the bass (barely grammar). Alternatively, the accompanist may just do the obvious and very effective thing by throwing his dominant five-three right in on top of the tonic six-four which is the actual as opposed to the contrived harmony of the voice (not grammar at all). And this is the preferred convention for opera wherever the drama has grown so tense that waiting for the standard convention gets to be intolerably dilatory, and hurrying the voice along is just what the situation may so often require.

Thus Heinichen *(302a)* in 1728 wanted 'recitative cadences always, I say always to resolve' after the singer except that 'in theatrical music . . . it can happen that one takes occasion to shorten the matter' (Ex. 170, and see Ex. 171 for Telemann). For Quantz *(302b)* in 1752 the bass 'must generally, at all cadences of theatrical recitative' whether with orchestral or continuo accompaniment, 'begin its two notes, which most often pass through a falling leap of a fifth, under the last syllable, and not strike them too slowly, but with liveliness'. For 'fiery recitative in opera', C. P. E. Bach *(302c)* in 1762 approved of a first harpsichordist who, to help bring in on time a dispersed orchestra, 'does not wait for the entire cadence of the singing part, but strikes already on the last syllable what should rightly come first on the following harmony'.

Instruments of accompaniment

The instruments and combinations used for continuo accompaniment during the baroque period were various, ranging from a single lute (taken over from one renaissance practice) to a small chamber group of perhaps strings, flutes, lutes and keyboards (as in French opera). But by the eighteenth century the standard continuo accompaniment was harpsichord or organ supported by a melodic bass instrument, itself optionally doubled where appropriate by a contra-bass instrument at the octave below. A keyboard alone was also acceptable, though not as a rule for preference except with obbligato keyboard parts as in the violin sonatas and gamba sonatas of J. S. Bach. A melodic bass alone was regarded as sufficient at need.

(303) A. Agazzari, Siena, 1607: 'As foundation, we have the instruments which hold together and support the whole consort of voices and instruments in the aforesaid Consort, as Organ, Harpsichord *etc.*, and, likewise, in the case of few or single Voices, Lute, Theorbo, Harp *etc.*

'As ornamentation, we have those which make playful melodies (scherzando) and counterpoints (contraponteggiando), thereby rendering the harmony more pleasant and resounding; as the Lute, Theorbo, Harp, Lirone [bass lyra or lyra da gamba], Cither, Spinet, Chitarrina [small Chitarone], Violin, Pandora. . . .

'When playing an instrument which functions as foundation, you must perform with great discretion, keeping your attention on the body of the voices; for if these are numerous, you must play full chords and draw more stops, but if they are few, you must reduce the stops and use few notes [*i.e.* in each chord], sounding the work as purely and correctly as possible, without indulging much in passage-work or florid movement (non passeggiando, ò rompendo molto); but on the contrary, sustaining the voices by sometimes reduplicating the bass in the double-bass register, and keeping out of the upper registers when the voices, especially the sopranos and the Falsettos, are employing them; at such times you must so far as possible try to keep off the same note which the Soprano sings, and avoid making florid divisions on it, so as not to reduplicate the voice part and cover the quality of that voice or the florid divisions which the good singer is making up there; whence it is desirable to play compact chords in a lower register (assai stretto, e grave). . . .

'[Of the instruments of ornamentation:] The instruments which blend in with the voices in a variety of ways, blend in with them for no other purpose, I think, than to add spice to (condire) the aforesaid consort: a harder matter, because as the foundation [instrumentalist] has to play [with mainly chordal harmony] the Bass as it stands in front of him, he does not need a great skill in counterpoint, whereas [the ornamenting instrumentalist] does need it, for he has to compose original parts, and original and diverse divisions and counterpoints upon that given bass.

'Thus whoever performs on the Lute, the noblest instrument of any, must perform nobly, with great fertility and diversity, yet not, like some who have an agile hand, making continual runs and divisions from start to finish, particularly in combination with other instruments all doing the same, which leaves nothing to be heard but noise and confusion, distasteful and distressing to the hearer.

'Chords should be struck at times, with restrained reiterations; at other times, florid passages both slow and fast should be executed, besides [thematic or canonic] points of imitation at different intervals of pitch and of time (in diverse corde, e lochi), together with ornaments such as *gruppi*, *trilli* and *accenti*. . . .

'The violin requires fine passages, long and clear, lively sections (scherzi), little replies, and fugal imitations repeated in several places, affecting appoggiaturas (accenti), nuances of bowing (? – arcate mute), gruppi, trilli, *etc.*

'The [great bass-viol, the Italian] *Violone*, proceeds gravely, as befits its position in the lowest register, supporting the harmony of the other parts with its mellow sonority, keeping on its thick strings as far as possible, and frequently doubling the Bass at the Octave below.'

(304) Michael Praetorius, Wolfenbüttel, 1619: 'When 2 or 3 voices sing accompanied by the general bass which the organist or lutanist has in front of him and from which he plays, it is very good, and indeed almost essential, to have this same general bass played in addition by some bass instrument, such as a bassoon, a dolcian, or a trombone, or best of all, on a violone.' [Violone here almost certainly means a cello of large size but at 8-ft, not 16-ft, pitch as the term sometimes implied in the eighteenth century.]

(305) [Peter Prelleur], London, 1730: 'Organo, signifies properly an Organ, but when it is written over any Piece of Musick, then it signifies the Thorough Bass' [leaving undetermined the actual choice of instruments].

(306) François Couperin, Paris, 1714: 'If we can join a gamba or a cello to the accompaniment of the organ or the harpsichord, that will be good.'

(307) C. P. E. Bach, Berlin, 1762: 'The organ is indispensable in church music on account of the fugues, loud choruses, and more generally, on account of the binding effect. . . . But whenever recitatives and arias are used in church, especially those whose inner parts accompany simply so as to leave the voice free to make ornamental variations, there must be a harpsichord. . . . This instrument is also essential in the theatre or in a room, on account of such arias and recitatives. . . . The most complete accompaniment to a solo, and the one to which no possible exception can be taken, is a keyboard instrument in combination with the violoncello.'

TABLE VI Forms of figuring

A. Figures in a form equivalent to an added sharp

$\dagger$ 2 4 5 6 7 8 9

2 5$^+$ 9

B. Figures in a form equivalent to an added natural

5‡

5$^+$

C. Figures in a form equivalent to an added flat

4 5 6 7 7 7 9

5

5

5

Examples of accompaniment

(308) D. Delair, Paris, 1690: 'One sometimes finds in opera basses, a flat, or a sharp, before a figure but the said flats or sharps, do not modify at all the said figures, they only indicate that the natural chord has to be major or minor.'

Ex. 158. Giacomo Carissimi, cantata, 'In un mar di pensieri' (mid 17th cent.), in London, Brit. Lib., MS R.M. 24, i. 11, No. 5, m. 29, misplaced accidental:

Ex. 159. Giacomo Carissimi, cantata, 'In un mar di pensieri' (mid 17th cent.), in Vienna, Nat. Lib., MS 17765, ff. 41–8v, (a) mm. 7–8, 6 for ♭ and ♭ for 6; (b) mm. 45–46, corresponding section correctly notated (this is an easily made and very common mistake):

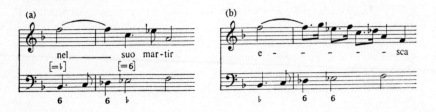

Ex. 160. (a) Jean-Baptiste Lully, *Cadmus et Hermione*, in the collected edition by Henry Prunières, Paris, 1930–9, Vol. I, p. 39, lead in bass notated in the printed ed. of 1674 but not in the MS score; (b) Marin Marais, *Alcione*, Paris, 1706, lead in bass notated (with under-dotting for convenience) in the printed short score, Paris, Bibl. Nat. Vm.² 204, p. 11, with the instruction 'Dernière Notte pour la Basse Continuo', but not in the MS full score, Vm.² 205, prepared for the revival of 1741, p. 10; (c) Jean-Philippe Rameau, *Hippolyte et Aricie*, Paris, [n.d.], 1st perf. 1733, pp. xx-xxi, bass as printed, (d) as written over in ink:

Ex. 161. Arcangelo Corelli, Trio Sonata Op. 11 No. 1, Corrente, section joins as realized by Robert Donington:

Ex. 162. Marin Marais, *Pièces à 1 et à 2 violes*, Paris, 1686, 2nd Suite, Sarabande, m. 8: (a) as written; (b) approximately as intended (my interpretation confirmed by the figuring; the commas are French signs for trills):

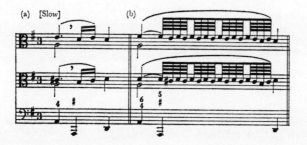

Ex. 163. (a) G. P. Telemann, *Generalbass-Übungen*, Hamburg, 1733–5, No. 36, harmony figured to accommodate implied cadential trill; (b) my interpretation:

Of No. 5, m. 8 (Ex. 164 below) Telemann writes: 'The $\frac{6}{4}$ in the right hand would be taken [although the figuring gives ♯] for [accommodating the] ornamentation, because of course the singer lets the g, as the 4, be heard strongly before the tr comes.' [That 'of course' (*doch*) confirms how unreservedly Telemann expected such a trill to be prepared by an upper note start strong enough, and long enough, to affect the harmony.]

Ex. 164. (a) G. P. Telemann, op. cit., No. 5, m. 8, his own figuring contravened in his realization to accommodate the implied cadential trill; (b) my interpretation:

Ex. 165 (i) and (ii). Johann David Heinichen, *General-Bass*, Dresden, 1728, (i) Pt. 1, Ch. VI, Sect. 39 and (ii) Pt. 1, Ch. VI, Sect. 31ff. figurations giving a good sonority on the harpsichord:

(i)

(ii)

(a) written:

(b) performed:

(c)

Ex. 166. Johann David Heinichen, *General-Bass*, Dresden, 1728, I, VI, 40, point of imitation as it can be introduced into the accompaniment by the performer:

Ex. 167. Alessandro Scarlatti, cantata, 'Da sventura a sventura', with freely contra-puntal realization (in Naples, Conservatorio, MS 34.5.2, ff. 2–6v and other MSS), probably by the composer and certainly contemporary:

Ex. 168. George Frideric Handel, Sonata in C major for Viola da Gamba, slow movement, plain text as notated; suggested free ornamentation by Robert Donington; notated accompaniment by Handel:

(first time: as notated by Handel)

(second time: as ornamented by R.D.)

(Handel's accompaniment: N.B. hold down all notes in the right hand till the harmony changes)

Ex. 169. George Frideric Handel, Trio Sonata in G minor, Op. 11 No. 8, 3rd movt., Largo, realization with persistent figuration (essentially broken chords) by Robert Donington:

Ex. 170. Johann David Heinichen, *General-Bass*, Dresden, 1728, II, i, 54, note dd (p. 674), on telescoped cadences, has the following illustrations, showing two barely grammatical and one ungrammatical (but in practice effective) harmonizations, for which see my p. 153 above:

Ex. 171. G. P. Telemann, *Singe-, Spiel- und Generalbass-Übungen*, Hamburg, 1733–34, No. 40, cadences recitative annotated 'these closes in opera would be struck immediately, while the singer speaks the last syllables, in cantatas however one must strike them afterwards':

Ex. 172. J. A. Scheibe in F. W. Marpurg's *Kritische Briefe*, Berlin, for 1760–62, p. 352, letter 109, warns us that 'some composers are in the habit of anticipating the penultimate note of the cadence, namely the dominant, without inserting the rest' required (and commonly prolonged) as at my p. 152 above, and as shown here by Scheibe with my interpretation:

Chapter Ten · The Sound

Sound and sense

And so we come to the last great quality of baroque style and performance to be considered in this book: the sound. The issues are complex, and will not be more than briefly touched on here; but the principle is simple. The *sound* of baroque music can only be recovered on its own instruments in original state, with the techniques and idioms of its original performers; the *style* is very largely dependent upon the sound.

We cannot be sure how closely we are recovering the baroque sound, since our evidence is not audible and conclusive as tape-recordings would be. We have craftsmen expert but not infallible in studying such instruments as survive sufficiently unaltered for the purpose; we can draw a few cautious conclusions from folk traditions; we have built up a body of experience consistent enough and convincing enough to make better sense of our familiar classics and to give greater pleasure from our unfamiliar rediscoveries, in performances of which the fresh colourings and open textures are unmistakably appropriate: not necessarily in every particular, but certainly for the general ambience. Putting aside so far as possible both our romantic and our pedantic preconceptions, we should indeed have the musicianship to feel our way into the artistic implications of what we do know; and while we are not always in agreement, the area of our agreement is nevertheless impressive. I see no reason to doubt that it is broadly valid.

We should not underestimate the present value of modern instruments in baroque music; but they offer no substitute for the natural match of sound with sense which comes from using baroque instruments. Merely by using a baroque-form bow we help ourselves towards baroque-style articulation: the implement is working for us. Gut strings are instructive, and so are baroque reeds or mouthpieces. To have actually played on baroque instruments may teach still better how to play modern instruments appropriately. To mix baroque with modern instruments invites problems of blend and balance and has limited advantages, beyond the obvious necessity for introducing the essential harpsichord. The most practical solution under favourable circumstances is to use baroque instruments entirely.

Where circumstances are environmentally or artistically or just humanly unfavourable, modern instruments may be preferred; or they may for various reasons be unavoidable. It is still open to the performers to cultivate a baroque style, using baroque techniques and idioms up to the point at which structural and acoustic differences intervene. It is remarkable how much improvement a good awareness of style can bring. It will not bring a baroque sound; but it may bring a fine sampling of baroque musicianship as this present book attempts to outline it. Other things being equal, the baroque sound will serve the music best, besides being often so very beautiful in itself. But then, so can a modern sound be very beautiful, and the decision is really one of what goes best with what.

In any one performance, the sound is the sense and the sense is the sound. But it does not follow that only one sound will do. There can sometimes be different sonorities, but equally appropriate. Thus much though not all baroque keyboard music was and is more or less interchangeable for harpsichord, clavichord or chamber organ; but English consorts scored in close counterpoint for low registers on the viols are too idiomatic to tolerate transcribing. J. S. Bach's unspecified *Art of Fugue* tolerates various modern scorings because of the more open lie of the counterpoint; but his unaccompanied violin suites are idiomatic for the violin, and properly speaking for the baroque violin at that.

The principle here is suitability. If the sound really suits the sense, the music is not misrepresented, even when it is differently presented. We shall not nowadays from choice substitute flutes for recorders in J. S. Bach's Fourth Brandenburg; but this substitution does not make a good performance impossible, as playing on either out of style must do. And when baroque title-pages stipulated a choice of soloists between violin, flute, recorder, oboe, etc., this was not only to sell more copies; a good working can often be made in more than one of these optional sonorities. Modern string tone, on the other hand, though it can be made far more suitable by appropriate handling, is different enough to be itself something of a transcription, which is not to everyone's satisfaction now, and may become much less so in the future. Suitability can obviously be a matter of degree, however, and it must be admitted that the performer matters even more than the instrument.

The instruments matter very largely because they are an aspect of the style. The right instruments will not play right for the wrong musicians. A fine performance on modern instruments may actually be more authentic than a weak performance on baroque instruments; for fine musicianship is also an aspect of authenticity. Style is the sum of which all aspects of authenticity are the parts, and style can only be achieved by the musicians, but best when working with the baroque instruments.

(309) *François Couperin, Paris, 1722:* These pieces [in the *Concerts Royaux*] 'suit not only the harpsichord, but also the violin, the flute, the oboe, the viol and the bassoon'.

Also Paris, 1722: 'These pieces [in the *Troisième Livre*] are indeed suitable for two flutes or oboes, as well as for two violins, two viols, and other instruments of equal pitch; it being understood that those who perform them adapt them to the range of theirs.'

Transparency and incisiveness

There are two basic characteristics of baroque sound which, under whatever conditions of performance, it is necessary to achieve: a transparent sonority, and an incisive articulation.

(i) By transparent sonority I mean a tone which lets the details through distinctly and does not fuse them into an atmospheric impression. Harpsichord tone, for example, is acoustically more transparent than piano tone because its upper harmonics are more widely spaced. Rapid and heavy bow strokes yield less transparency than strokes of a moderate speed and pressure; rapid but light strokes yield less solidity. Heavy vibrato thickens the tone, whereas moderate vibrato colours it without endangering transparency. Simply too much volume may diminish the transparency by prolonging the confusing reverberation of a resonant hall. Even at climaxes, a certain ease and relaxation should be sparing us any feeling of unnatural strain. In baroque music a thick sonority cannot be suitable; a ringing sonority may be very suitable indeed.

(ii) By an incisive articulation I mean using crisp accents and sharp attacks rather than explosive accents or massive attacks. A smooth cantabile may be justifiable, or an etched détaché, or any requisite combination or modification of these; but very seldom a weighty *sforzando*. A harpsichord, again, is by nature adapted to this range of desirable articulations, though not to much dynamic nuance of individual notes. A violin, baroque or modern, is supremely adapted to dynamic nuance, but often serves baroque articulation better by the bite rather than by the weight of the bow. Other instruments including woodwind and brass can likewise etch their definition. Unrelieved legato is undesirable, because there are always the phrasings and the patterns which must divide it up. Unrelieved staccato is equally improbable, because there are always the subtle groupings which require some notes to be a little more or less prolonged or joined or stressed than others. A line which is too monotonous and unfeeling is just as bad as a line which is too emphasized and restless. In baroque music, a ponderous articulation can hardly be suitable; a lively articulation may be very suitable indeed.

The voice throughout (and indeed before and after) the baroque period used the Italian bel canto technique. The placing is very far forward, right up in the mask; the support is from the muscles of the trunk including the diaphragm; the chest is used for raw colouring low down, and carried as high as possible up into the head voice, with the registers fully contrasted though smoothly joined. The forward placing not only projects the tone but makes the words audible as no other vocal technique can do. It also conduces both to agility and to good intonation.

(310) Giovanni Maffei, Naples, 1562: The chief source of the voice is 'the motive power of the chest'; use 'a sound produced by the minute and controlled reverberation of the air in the throat . . . extend the tongue so that the tip reaches and touches the roots of the teeth below . . . hold the mouth open, and exactly no more than it is held when one talks with friends . . . push the breath with the voice little by little, and be very careful that it does not come out through the nose, or through the palate . . . frequent those who sing in the throat with much fluency'.

Claudio Monteverdi *(311)* in 1610 admired 'a fine voice, strong and long' because produced by 'singing in the chest'. Vincenzo Giustiniani *(312)* in 1628 wrote: 'diminish and increase the voice loudly or softly . . . now with dragging, now dividing . . . and pronouncing the words distinctly in such a manner that one might hear even the last syllable of every word, not interrupted or suppressed by passages or other ornaments'. Ignazio Donati *(313)* required 'the mouth half open so as not to lose so much breath'. Pier Francesco Tosi *(314)* at Bologna in 1723 wrote 'unite the [head voice] with the chest voice' to make a perfect join [while neglecting neither]. Joachim Quantz *(315)* in his autobiographical note of 1755 wrote of the tenor Paita that his voice 'would not have been by nature so fine and even, if he himself, through art, had not known how to join the chest voice with the head voice'. Charles Burney *(316)* in 1773 wrote both of Senesino and of Orsino as making the most rapid ornamentation 'always from the breast'. Giambattista Mancini *(317)* in 1774 above all advised the singer never under any provocation to yield to 'forcing the voice'. If the voice is properly produced on this forward bel canto method, there is no need to do so, even in a large hall against an orchestra. The voice will cut through because of the purity and not the violence of the vibrations.

Similar considerations apply to strings and wind. The volume will be a little less on baroque than on modern instruments, but will carry well if the vibrations are pure because accurately focused. In either case it is this sharply focused sound which is required, both in *piano* and *forte*. For string players in particular, this means playing well into the string, with ample pressure for the volume desired, but not too much speed of the bow. Circumstances vary, of course, but it is quite often good advice just to use a little more pressure and a little less bow.

Gut strings, uncovered except for the lowest, bring a great improvement in sonority: and a baroque-style bow makes baroque articulation not only approximately but wholly possible, and is (compared with a baroque violin) a relatively inexpensive and most advisable investment. It probably makes more technical and acoustic difference than the baroque violin itself. Chin-rests were not in use, but appear to make a technical rather than an acoustic difference; end-pins are occasionally shown in baroque pictures, and appear to make no acoustic difference. To hold the violin against the shoulder is fully authenticated, and may be tried for the technical challenge and instruction which it imposes; but to steady the violin under the chin or cheek is also unmistakably authenticated pictorially and descriptively, and is certainly more convenient, except perhaps for dance music and similar music in the first position where no difficulty in shifting down occurs.

There is likewise good descriptive and pictorial evidence both for holding the bow at the nut (as in modern practice) and for holding it a few inches away from the nut (which gives a different balance preferred by some specialists today). The average baroque bow is in any case a little shorter than the modern standard, and can perhaps more effectively be used at full length if held at the nut (the shorter hold may indeed be tried for fast passages). For short strokes continued over an extended passage, the most generally suitable part of the bow is likely to be just above the middle, since at the point they may sound too insubstantial, and at the heel too massive, particularly if taken off the string (not a baroque technique). It is generally best to use a baroque bow at fairly tight tension.

Chords of more notes than two are not meant to be forcibly held down but tactfully arpeggiated, as Jean-Philippe Rameau *(318)* explained at Paris in 1741: 'stopping on that' note 'from the side of which the melody continues; or one gives the preference, sometimes to the notes at the top, sometimes those at the bottom'. Jean-Jacques Rousseau *(319)* confirmed at Paris in 1768 this standard 'manner of performing in rapid succession the different notes' of a chord on the violin, cello or viol 'because the convexity of the bridge prevents the bow from pressing on all the strings at once' (i.e. except by a degree of pressure which sounds too strenuous for baroque music, including the unaccompanied violin and cello suites of J. S. Bach). The note which starts the arpeggio, not the note which ends it, will normally though not invariably take the beat.

It must not be thought, however, that robust playing was excluded: 'draw an honest and manly tone from the violin', Leopold Mozart (320) recommended at Augsburg in 1756; 'you should not confine yourself to the point of the bow with a certain kind of rapid stroke which hardly presses on to the string, but must always play solidly. . . . We must manage the bow from loud to soft in such a way that a good, steady, singing, and as it were round, fat tone can always be heard'. True, 'moving in our mournful airs', and 'tender', are descriptions applied to the transverse flute by François Raguenet (321) at Paris in 1702; but Marin Mersenne (322) at Paris in 1636 called the shawms 'proper for large assemblies . . . on account of the great noise which they produce . . . for they have the most powerful tone of all instruments, and the most violent, except for the trumpet'. The oboe family which replaced the shawms was much refined by the French makers later in the seventeenth century; but François Raguenet (323) at Paris in 1702 still called them 'equally mellow and piercing', with 'infinitely the advantage of the violins in all brisk, lively airs'. Jean-Laurent de Béthizy (324) at Paris in 1754 wrote that 'the sound of the oboe is gay and is particularly suited to open-air entertainment', and of the bassoon as 'strong and brusque' yet also capable of 'very sweet, very gracious and very tender sounds . . . there is no more beautiful accompaniment than those in which the composer knows how to mingle tastefully the sounds of one or more bassoons with those of violins and flutes'.

Modern work on baroque reed instruments confirms the impression that a somewhat edgy sound was favoured, of which the effect in a baroque orchestra is excellently colourful when the reed is right. Both oboes and bassoons should double the strings extensively even where not specified, since we meet instructions such as 'the oboes' or 'the bassoons are silent' in passages where there is no other indication that they should previously have been playing. Doubling the bass-line with bassoons is particularly well authenticated and advantageous in Handel; it is a valid scoring in many baroque orchestral situations. Trumpet parts are commonly but not necessarily specified where appropriate. The use of trumpets implies the use of kettle-drums, since their performers belonged to the same ceremonial corps, frequently loaned for musical occasions. The baroque trumpet could 'imitate the softest echo', as Marin Mersenne (325) remarked at Paris in 1636; its agility in its high registers reached a degree of virtuosity to which many notated obbligatos bear evidence, where it cannot have been used at great volume but rather for its silvery brilliance. That would, indeed, be quite in keeping with a certain baroque inclination to delicacy of timbre, though we should never assume that baroque musicians were reticent where the occasion arose for ample contrasts of volume. Mere scaling down is not a test of authenticity. Transparency and incisiveness are the proper tests.

A balance in music and performance

Of all the qualities of baroque style and performance touched upon in this book, perhaps the most attractive to our generation is their fluid character. So far from being, as once was thought, a rigid discipline, rhythmically strict and sonorously monotonous, baroque music abounds in variability. Beneath the symmetry, the flexibility; behind the scanty notation, the performer's open options. Order and proportion, though unquestionably relevant, are only half the story of baroque music; the other half is impetuosity and fantasy.

Just such a balance of qualities may serve us in our performances today. Not a surcharge of misplaced weightiness. Not an undercharge of insufficient vital energy. Simply a normal flow of musical enjoyment in sufficient awareness of the appropriate techniques and idioms.

References

(1) Sir Thomas More, *Utopia*, in Latin, Louvain, 1516, Eng. trans. Ralph Robinson, London, 1551, Bk. II., cited from Everyman ed., London, 1910, p. 109

(2) Baldassare Castiglione, *Il libro del cortegiano*, Venice, 1528, ed. B. Maier, Turin, 1955, pp. 147–8, Eng. trans. Sir Thomas Hoby as *The Courtyer of Count Baldassar Castilio*, London, 1561, cited from Everyman ed. as *The Book of the Courtier*, London, 1928, p. 61

(3) Richard Hooker, *Laws of Ecclesiastical Polity*, Bk. V, London, cited from 1597, Everyman ed., London, 1907, p. 146

(4) Charles Butler, *The Principles of Musik, in Singing and Setting*, London, 1636, p. 1

(5) Sir Thomas Browne, *Religio Medici*, London, 1642, cited from Everyman ed., London, 1906, p. 79

(6) Thomas Mace, *Musick's Monument*, London, 1676, p. 19

(7) Angelo Berardi, *Ragionamenti musicali*, Bologna, 1681, p. 87

(8) [L'abbé François Raguenet] *Paralele des italiens et des françois, en ce qui regarde la musique et les opéra*, Paris, 1702, [misprinted as 1602], Eng. trans. ?by J. E. Galliard as *A Comparison between the French and Italian Musick and Opera's*, London, 1709, cited from *Musical Quarterly*, XXXII, 3 (July 1946), p. 422

(9) François Couperin, *L'Art de toucher le clavecin*, Paris, 1716 (mainly known in enl. ed., Paris, 1717), preface

(10) Johann David Heinichen, *Der General-Bass in der Composition*, Dresden, 1728, Introd., p. 24

(11) Francesco Geminiani, *A Treatise of Good Taste in the Art of Musick*, London, 1749, p. 4

(12) Friedrich Wilhelm Marpurg, *Der critische Musicus an der Spree*, Berlin, 2 Sept. 1749

(13) Joachim Quantz, *Versuch einer Anweisung die Flöte traversiere zu spielen*, Berlin, 1752, XVIII, 28; the Fr. ed. as *Essai d'une methode pour apprendre à jouer de la flute traversiere*, Berlin, 1752, was authorized, in the preface, by Quantz himself.

(14) Carl Philipp Emanuel Bach, *Versuch über die wahre Art das Clavier zu spielen*, Berlin, 1753, III, 13. (Part II is Berlin, 1762.)

(15) Charles Burney, *The Present State of Music in Germany*, London, 1773, II, p. 156

(16) Marin Mersenne, *Harmonie universelle*, 2 pts., Paris, 1636–7, II, vi, 356

(17) Georg Muffat, *Florilegium*, I, Augsburg, 1695, preface

(18) As *(8)*, pp. 415ff.

(19) Roger North, *The Autobiography of Roger North*, [c.1695], ed. A. Jessopp, London, 1887, Sect. 114

(20) Pier Francesco Tosi, *Opinioni de' cantori antichi, e moderni*, Bologna, 1723, Eng. trans. by J. E. Galliard as *Observations on the Florid Song*, London, 1742, p. 92

(21) As *(10)*, p. 92

(22) As *(13)*, X, 19; XVIII, 53; XVII, vii, 12; XI, 9

(23) Thomas Morley, *A Plaine and Easie Introduction to Practicall Musicke*, 1597, p. 9

(24) Gioseffo Zarlino, *Le istitutioni harmoniche*, Venice, 1558, ed. of 1562, p. 278

(25) As *(23)*

(26) Pierre Maillart, *Les tons, ou discours, sur les modes de musique*, Tournai, 1610, p. 349

(27) Athanasius Kircher, *Musurgia universalis*, 2 vols., Rome, 1650, pp. 676, 679, 684

(28) John Playford, *A Breefe Introduction to the Skill of Musick for Song and Violl*, London, 1654 [nineteen numbered and several unnumbered editions, with varying contents and slightly varying titles, to 1730], pp. 15–17, 25ff.

(29) Christopher Simpson, *The Principles of Practical Musick*, London, 1665 [later eds with varying contents and titles], p. 19; ed. of 1706, pp. 12, 22

(30) As *(17)*

(31) Charles Masson, *Nouveau traité des regles de la composition de la musique*, Paris, 1697, 2nd ed. 1699, p. 6

(32) Étienne Loulié, *Elements ou principes de musique*, Paris, 1696, p. 69

(33) As *(10)*, Pt. I, Ch. IV, Sect. 48–50, pp. 348ff.; Sect. 38 (fn), p. 333

(34) As *(33)*, Sect. 37

(35) As *(13)*, V, 13

(36) Leopold Mozart, *Versuch einer gründlichen Violinschule*, Augsburg, 1756, I, ii, 5

(37) As *(29)*, I, 10, 37; and see eds of 1706 and after, p. 23, p. 25

(38) Alexander Malcolm, *A Treatise of Musick, Speculative, Practical, and Historical*, Edinburgh, 1721, p. 394

(39) James Grassineau, *A Musical Dictionary*, London, 1740, under 'Allegro'. [Largely but not wholly pirated from *(41)* below]

(40) Henry Purcell (or ? his editor posthumously), *A Choice Collection of Lessons for the Harpsichord or Spinet*, London, 1696, preface

(41) Sébastien de Brossard, *Dictionnaire des termes*, Paris, 1701, but almost entirely extant in its enlarged version as *Dictionaire de musique*, Paris, 1703

(42) As *(38)*, p. 395

(43) As *(39)*

(44) C. P. E. Bach and Johann Friedrich Agricola, joint article in Lorenz Mizler's *Musikalische Bibliothek*, Leipzig, 1739–54, IV, 1, p. 171 (and see *(214)* below)

(45) As *(13)*, XII, 2

(46) As *(14)*, III, 10

(47) As *(36)*, I, iii, 27, and I, ii, 7

(48) Meredith Ellis and Wendy Hilton, the former a musicologist-dancer and the latter a dancer-musicologist (see her *Dance of Court and Theatre*, New York, 1977), are among those most active and successful in this valuable line of approach, previously opened up by Mabel Dolmetsch in conjunction with the pioneer researches of Arnold Dolmetsch

(49) Some introductory material is in John Guthrie, *Historical Dances for the Theatre: The Pavan and the Minuet*, Worthing, 1950; and rather more in Mabel Dolmetsch, *Dances of England and France from 1450 to 1600*, London, 1949, and *Dances of Spain and Italy from 1400 to 1600*, London, 1954. Some of the best source material is in Thoinot Arbeau [i.e. Jehan Tabourot], *Orchesographie*, Langres, 1589; Fabritio Caroso, *Nobiltà di dame*, Venice, 1600, and Jean-Philippe Rameau, *Le maître à danser*, Paris, 1726

(50) As *(41)*

(51) Jean-Jacques Rousseau, *Dictionnaire de musique*, Paris, 1768; also Amsterdam, 1768; but supposed prior publication has not been confirmed, though the Paris preface is dated 20 Dec. 1764 and pre-publication copies have been reported

(52) As *(6)*, pp. 129ff.

(53) Johann Gottfried Walther, *Musicalisches Lexicon*, Leipzig, 1732

(54) As *(52)*

(55) As *(31)*, pp. 7ff.

(56) Paris, Bibl. Nat., Rés. Vm^7. 675, f.57v.

(57) As *(41)*

(58) As *(53)*

(59) As *(13)*, XVII, vii, 58

(60) As *(29)*

(61) As *(38)*

(62) Michel L'Affilard, *Principes tres-faciles pour bien apprendre la musique*, Paris, 1694, from 5th ed. of Paris, 1705 onwards. See Erich Schwandt, 'L'Affillard's Published "Sketchbooks"', *Musical Quarterly*, 63 (1977), p. 102

(63) As·*(32)*

(64) William Tans'ur, *A New Musical Grammar*, London, 1746

(65) [Henri Louis Choquel], *La musique rendue sensible . . .* , Paris, 1759

(66) As *(13)*, XVII, vii, 49ff.

(67) Neal A. Zaslaw, in 'Materials for the Life and Works of Jean-Marie Leclair l'aîné', Ph.D. diss., Columbia Univ., 1970

(68) Anton Bemetzrieder, *Leçons de clavecin, et principes d'harmonie*, Paris, 1771, p. 68

(69) Girolamo Frescobaldi, *Toccate e partite d'intavolatura di cimbalo . . . Libro primo*, Rome, 1615; 2nd ed., Rome 1615–16, preface

(70) As *(6)*, p. 81

(71) Jean Rousseau, *Traité de la viole*, Paris, 1687, p. 60

(72) As *(9)*, p. 38

(73) As *(13)*, XI, 13

(74) As *(14)*, III, 28

(75) As *(13)*, XI, 13

(76) As *(14)*, III, 8 and 28

(77) As *(76)*, but add ed. of 1787, III, 28; also XXXI, 3; also Part II, Berlin, 1762, XXIX, 20

(78) Matthew Locke's music for Shadwell's adaptation of Shakespeare's *The Tempest*, perf. London, 1675, publ. in *The English Opera . . . to which is Adjoyned the Instrumental Musick in The Tempest*, London, 1675

(79) Severo Bonini, *Affetti spirituali*, Venice, 1615, notice at end of both soprano parts

(80) Claudio Monteverdi, of the 'Lettera amorosa', *Settimo libro de madrigali*, Venice, 1619; and of the song 'Non havea Febo ancora', *Madrigali guerrieri et amorosi . . . in genere rappresentativo . . . Libro ottavo*, Venice, 1638

(81) Giovanni Battista Doni, 'Trattato della musica scenica' [*c.*1635], in *De' trattati di musica di Gio. Battista Doni*, II, ed. A. F. Gori, Florence, 1763, Appendix [i.e. first draft of the 'Trattato'], p. 23

(82) Giovanni Bonachelli, *Corona di sacri gigli*, Venice, 1642, Preface

(83) As *(7)*, p. 136

(84) As *(41)*, under RECITATIVO

(85) Johann Mattheson, *Der vollkommene Capellmeister*, Hamburg, 1739, Pt. II, Ch. 13, Sect. 26ff. (pp. 214ff.)

(86) As *(14)*, Pt. II, Berlin, 1762, XXXVIII, 2

(87) As *(13)*, XVII, vii, 53

(88) As *(44)*

(89) [Henri Louis Choquel] *La musique rendue sensible . . .* , Paris, 1759, 2nd ed. of Paris, 1762, pp. 109ff., 118

(90) As *(31)*

(91) [Borin,?] *Le musique theorique, et pratique, dans son ordre naturel*, Paris, 1722, p. 29

(92) Michel de Saint-Lambert, *Nouveau traité de l'accompagnement*, Paris, 1707, p. 25

(93) As *(51)*, under 'Chaconne'

(94) As *(41)*

(95) As *(39)*

(96) As *(45)*

(97) As *(46)*

(98) As *(9)*

(99) As *(9)*, p. 61

(100) J. S. Bach, 'Inventionen und Sinfonien' of 1723, sub-title

(101) As *(69)*

(102) As *(6)*, p. 109

(103) As *(9)*, p. 10

(104) As *(13)*, VI, 10; XI, 10, 19; XII, 4

(105) As *(14)*, III, 5

(106) Friedrich Wilhelm Marpurg, *Anleitung zum Clavierspielen*, Berlin, 1755, 2nd ed. of 1765, I, vii, p. 29

(107) Giulio Caccini, *Le nuove musiche*, Florence, 1602, preface, trans. in Playford, as *(28)*, ed. of 1674, p. 40. [Not 1601, as title-page – not even Old Style; actual publication was delayed, and imprimaturs are dated June and July 1602, licence to print June *(sic)* 1602]

(108) Domenico Mazzocchi, *Dialoghi e sonetti*, Rome, 1638, preface

(109) Christopher Simpson, *Division-Violist*, London, 1659, 2nd ed. (as *Division Viol*), 1667, p. 10

(110) As *(6)*, p. 130

(111) As *(78)*

(112) W[olfgang] M[ichael] M[ylius], *Rudamenta musices*, [Gotha] 1685 (but most surviving copies are Gotha, 1686), p. 49

(113) As *(19)*, Sect. 106

(114) As *(8)*, pp. 426 and 429

(115) Alessandro Scarlatti, Letter to Prince Ferdinando de' Medici, 29 May 1706, in the Archivio di Stato di Firenzi, *Mediceo*, Filza 5903, letter No. 204

(116) Scipione di Maffei, 'Nuova invenzione d'un gravicembalo', *Giornale dei Letterati d'Italia*, v, Venice, 1711, p. 144

(117) As *(13)*, XI, 14

(118) As *(13)*, XVIII, vi, 12–17; esp. 14

(119) As *(14)*, III, 29

(120) As *(107)*

(121) Girolamo Fantini da Spoleti, *Modo per imparare a sonare di tromba*, Frankfurt am Main, 1638, pp. 6ff.

(122) As *(14)*, Pt. II, XXIX, 13

(123) Francesco Geminiani, *The Art of Playing on the Violin*, London, 1751, p. 8

(124) As *(36)*, v, 3

(125) David D. Boyden, *The History of Violin Playing from Its Origins to 1761 and Its Relationship to the Violin and Violin Music*, London, 1965, pp. 393ff.

(126) Giuseppe Tartini, *Lettera del defonto signor Giuseppe Tartini alla signora Maddelena Lombardini . . .*, Venice, 1770. [Letter of Padua, 5 March 1760]

(127) Charles Burney, trans. of the above as *A Letter from the Late Signor Tartini to Signora Maddelena Lombardini . . .*, London, 1771, 2nd ed. 1779, 3rd ed. as *An Important Lesson to Performers on the Violin*, London, 1879

(128) Sol Babitz, 'Differences between 18th-Century and Modern Violin Bowing', *The Score*, March 1957

(129) John Hsu, 'The Use of the Bow in French Solo Viol Playing of the 17th and 18th Centuries', *Early Music*, VI, 4 (Oct. 1978) pp. 526–9

(130) Cited from Hubert le Blanc, *Défense de la basse de viole contre les entreprises du violon et les prétensions du violoncel*, Amsterdam, 1740

(131) Sylvestro di Ganassi, *Regola Rubertina*, Venice, 1542, Ch. 11 (Pt 11 as *Lettione seconda . . .*, Venice, 1543)

(132) Martin Agricola, *Musica instrumentalis deudsch*, Wittenberg, last and different ed. of 1645, pp. 42–3

(133) As *(220)*, III, p. 231

(134) As *(16)*, trans. R. E. Chapman, The Hague, 1957, Bk 11, Sect. on lute ornaments, p. 24, p. 109

(135) Christopher Simpson, *Division Violist*, London, 1659, 1, 16

(136) As *(6)*, p. 109

(137) As *(71)*, pp. 100–1

(138) As *(123)*, p. 8

(139) As *(36)*, XI, iff.

(140) Lodovico Zacconi, *Prattica di musica*, Venice, 1592, LXVI, p. 59. (Pt 11 is Venice, 1622)

(141) As *(13)*, XII, 23; XVI, 24

(142) Charles Avison, *An Essay on Musical Expression*, London, 1752, p. 128

(143) [Abbé Marc-Antoine Laugier] *Apologie de la musique françoise, contre M. Rousseau*, [Paris] 1754, p. 59

(144) As *(36)*, XII, 13

(145) As *(123)*, p. 9

(146) As *(36)*, IV, 23

(147) For black notation as an aspect of 'coloration' remaining over from mensural notation, and for the occasional use of this to indicate the hemiola in baroque music, see Robert Donington, *The Interpretation of Early Music, New Version*, London, 1974, pp. 654ff.

(148) Loys Bourgeois, *Le droit chemin de musique*, Geneva, 1550, x

(149) Fray Tomás de Santa María, *Libro llamado Arte de tañer fantasía*, Valladolid, 1565, '7th condition'

(150) As *(69)*

(151) Giovanni Domenico Puliaschi, *Musiche varie a una voce*, Rome, 1618, 'L' autore a i lettori', last page

(152) Anonymous English MS c.1660–70, 'Miss Mary Burwell's Instruction Book for the Lute', ed. Thurston Dart, *Galphin Society Journal*, XI, 1958, pp. 3–62: see pp. 46–7

(153) Bénigne de Bacilly, *Remarques curieuses sur l'art de bien chanter*, Paris, 1668, p. 232

(154) Roger North, various unsorted and largely overlapping notes in the British Library, London, from about 1690 to about 1726; selection and edition by John Wilson as *Roger North on Music*, London, 1959, p. 223

(155) Alessandro Scarlatti, *Pirro e Demetrio*, perf. Naples, 1694, II, xvi

(156) As *(17)*

(157) As *(32)*, p. 38

(158) As *(41)*, under ANDANTE

(159) Michel de Saint-Lambert, *Les Principes du clavecin*, Paris, 1702, p. 25

(160) Hotteterre le Romain [Jacques Martin], *Principes de la flute traversiere . . .*, Paris, 1707, p. 24

(161) Michel Pignolet de Montéclair, *Nouvelle methode pour aprendre la musique*, Paris, 1709, p. 15

(162) As *(9)*, p. 38

(163) Pier Francesco Tosi, *Opinioni de' cantori antichi, e moderni,* Bologna, 1723, p. 114

(164) Michel Pignolet de Montéclair, *Petite methode pour apprendre la musique aux enfans et même aux personnes plus avancées en âge,* Paris [c.1730], p. 42

(165) [Michel Corrette], *Methode pour apprendre aisément à jouer de la flute traversiere,* Paris and Lyon [c.1740], p. 4

(166) Michel Corrette, *Methode, théorique et pratique pour apprendre en peu de tems le violoncelle,* Paris, 1741, pp. 4ff.

(167) As *(13)*, XI, 12 (for [a] to [c]); XVII, ii, 16 (for [d]). [My translation is adapted slightly to the French version, mainly to the German, both being of equal authority and published in the same place and year]

(168) As *(14)*, III, 27

(169) Nicolas Gigault, *Livre de musique,* Paris, 1683, preface

(170) Michel L'Affilard, *Principes tres-faciles pour bien apprendre la musique,* Paris, 1694, p. 30

(171) As *(32)*, p. 16

(172) Jacques Martin Hotteterre, *Méthode pour la musette,* Paris, 1737, p. 35

(173) Johann Mattheson, *Kern melodischer Wissenschaft,* Hamburg, 1737, p. 47

(174) As *(13)*, V, 21; XII, 24; XVII, vii, 58; XVII, ii, 16

(175) As *(14)*, Pt I, III, 23; Pt II, XXIV, 15; Pt I, III, 23 again; ed. of 1787 for last sentence cited

(176) As *(36)*, I, iii, 9–10

(177) Johann Abraham Peter Schultz, in Johann Georg Sulzer, *Allgemeine Theorie der schonen Kunste . . . Erster Theil, von A bis J [-zweiter Theil, von K bis Z],* Leipzig, 1771 [–1774], under 'Ouverture'

(178) Giannantonio Banner, *Compendio musico,* II, Padua, 1745, p. 111

(179) Michael B. Collins, 'The Performance of Triplets in the 17th and 18th Centuries', *Journ. Amer. Mus. Soc.,* XIX, 3 (Fall 1966), pp. 281–328

(180) Pietro Aaron, *Thoscanello de la musica,* Venice, 1523, p. 1 of the additions following Ch. 41

(181) Stephano Vanneo, MS treatise, 1531, trans. Vincentio Rosseto, *Recanetum de musica aurea,* Rome, 1533, III, 37

(182) As *(24)*, ed. of 1589, III, 252

(183) As *(23)*, p. 88

(184) Agostino Agazzari, *Del sonare sopra'l basso con tutti li stromenti e dell'uso loro nel conserto,* Siena, 1607, p. 6

(185) Francesco Bianciardi, *Breve regola per impar' a sonare sopra il basso con ogni sorte d'istrumento,* Siena, 1697, second of the nine rules

(186) Crescentio Sabrilli, *Il primo libro de madrigali a cinque voci,* Naples, 1611, preface

(187) Domenico Mazzocchi, *Partitura de' madrigali a cinque voci,* Rome, 1638, preface

(188) Wolfgang Ebner, trans. Johann Andreas Herbst in his *Arte prattica e poëtica,* Frankfurt, 1653, Rule 8

(189) As *(29)*, ed. of 1732, p. 5 (but other eds. have it)

(190) Lorenzo Penna, *Primi albori musicali*, Bologna, 1672, Bk. III, Ch. V, Second Rule

(191) Friedrich Erhard Niedt, *Musikalische Handleitung*, I, Hamburg, 1700, Ch. VIII, Rule 6

(192) As *(32)*, p. 11; see the trans., with additions and collations from the ed. of Amsterdam, 1698, by Albert Cohen, New York, 1965, including an unpublished MS Supplément, pp. 49–50 in Albert Cohen's ed.

(193) As *(123)*, p. [3]

(194) Daniel Gottlob Türk, *Klavierschule, oder Anweisung zum Klavierspielen für Lehrer und Lernende*, Leipzig and Halle, 1789, p. 46

(195) Jacopo Peri, *Euridice*, Florence, 1600, 'Avvertimento' (preface)

(196) Charles Burney, *A General History of Music, from the Earliest Ages to the Present Period*, 4 vols., London, 1776–89. Cited from ed. by F. Mercer, 2 vols., London, 1935 (repr. New York, 1957), p. 352

(197) Diego Ortiz, *Trattado de glosas sobre clausulas*, Rome, 1553, Introd.

(198) Hermann Finck, *Practica musica*, Wittenberg, 1556, Lib. V, [p. 8]

(199) Giovanni Camillo Maffei, *Delle lettere . . . v'è un discorso della voce*, comp. Don Valerio de' Paoli (Naples, 1562), Bk. I, pp. 5–81: Letter I, to Count d'Altavilla. Ed. in N. Bridgman, 'Giovanni Camillo Maffei et sa lettre sur le chant', *Revue de musicologie*, XXXVIII (July 1955) pp. 10–34

(200) As *(140)*, LXVI, pp. 58ff.

(201) As *(195)*

(202) As *(107)*

(203) As *(184)*, pp. 3ff.

(204) Scipione Cerreto, *Dell' arbore musicale*, Naples, 1608, p. 41

(205) Bartolomeo Barbarino, *Il secondo libro delli motetti . . . da cantarsi a una voce sola*, Venice, 1614, preface

(206) Enrico Radesca, *Il quinto libro delle canzonette, madrigali et arie, a tre, a una et a due voci*, Venice, 1617, preface

(207) Vincenzo Giustiniani, *Discorso sopra la musica* [1628], ed. in Angelo Solerti, *Le origini de melodramma*, Turin, 1903, p. 108

(208) As *(81)*, II, p. 69

(209) Pietro della Valle, 'Della musica del' età nostra', 1640, quoted in Angelo Solerti, *Le origini del melodramma*, Turin, 1903, pp. 159–160

(210) As *(153)*, pp. 135, 224

(211) Jean-Baptiste Lully, cited (purportedly) by Le Cerf de la Viéville, in J. Bonnet, *Histoire de la musique*, here quoted from ed. of Amsterdam, 1725, pp. 195ff.; but the passage as a whole stems from Le Cerf's *Comparison de la musique italienne et de la musique française*, Brussels, 1704–6, and also appears in shorter but otherwise almost identical form in [Nicolas Boindin], *Lettres historiques sur tous les spectacles de Paris, Seconde partie*, Paris, 1719, pp. 87ff.

(212) Roger North, Brit. Lib. MS Add. 32533, f.106v (English early 18th cent.). And see *(154)*

(213) Johann Adolf Scheibe, *Der critische Musicus*, 2 Vols., Hamburg, 1738–40 (also weekly but irregularly, 1737–40); I (1737) 6

(214) Johann Abraham Birnbaum, reply to *(212)* in Lorenz Christoph Mizler, *Neu eröffnete musikalische Bibliothek*, 4 Vols., Leipzig, 1739–54 (Vol. I was issued in 6 pts., 1736–8; Vol. II in 4 pts., 1740–43; Vol. III in 4 pts., 1746–52; of Vol. IV only Pt. I was pub., 1754): Leipzig, April, 1738, I, iv

(215) [John Hawkins] *Memoirs of the Life of Sig. Agostino Steffani*, [? London, c.1750], p. ii

(216) As *(20)*, p. 93

(217) As *(13)*, *[a]* XIII, 7; *[b]* XII, 26; *[c]* XII, 27; *[d]* XI, 6; *[e]* X, 13; *[f]* XVI, 24; *[g]* XVI, 26; *[h]* XVI, 27; *[i]* XV, 1; *[j]* XV, 5; *[k]* XV, 8; *[l]* XV, 17

(218) As *(39)*, under 'Fioretti'

(219) As *(51)*, under 'Passage'

(220) Michael Praetorius, *Syntagma musicum*, 3 Vols., Wittenberg and Wolfenbüttel, 1614–20 (orig. pub. I, I, Wolfenbüttel, 1614; I, 2, Wittenberg, 1615; II, Wolfenbüttel, 1618; III, Wolfenbüttel, 1618. But most surviving copies: I, Wittenberg, 1615; II, entitled 'Organographia', Wolfenbüttel, 1619 *(Theatrum instrumentorum, 1620);* III, Wolfenbüttel, 1619. Praetorius, however, merely gave a German version of Agazzari, for which see *(184)*

(221) As *(153)*

(222) The most thorough study comes in Frederick Neumann, *Ornamentation in Baroque and Post-Baroque Music, with Special Emphasis on J. S. Bach*, Princeton, 1978

(223) As *(196)*, II, p. 545

(224) Charles Burney, in Rees's *Cyclopaedia*, London, 1819, under 'Adagio'

(225) Adrianus Petit Coclico, *Compendium musices*, Nuremberg, 1552, first example

(226) As *(71)*, p. 72

(227) As *(92)*, Ch. VIII, Sect. 13, esp. p. 6

(228) François Couperin, *Pièces de clavecin, Troisième livre*, Paris, 1722, preface

(229) As *(213)*, 2nd ed., Leipzig, 1745, art. 78

(230) As *(13)*, VIII, 19

(231) As *(14)*, First Part: *[a]* II, i, 4; *[b]* II, i, 25; *[c]* III, 7; *[d]* II, i. 8; *[e]* II, i, 19; *[f]* II, i, 9; *[g]* II, i, 28; *[h]* II, i, 17; *[i]* II, i, 23; *[j]* II, i, 24

(232) Friedrich Wilhelm Marpurg, *Historisch-kritische Beyträge zur Aufnahme der Musik*, 5 Vols., Berlin, 1755–8 (and Supplement, Berlin, 1760), III, 1756, 2; and as *(106)*, I, ix, 3, p. 44

(233) As *(13)*, VIII, 7–9

(234) As *(123)*, p. 7

(235) J. E. Galliard, footnote to his trans. of Tosi, as *(20)*, p. 32

(236) As *(14)*, II, ii, 11 and 16

(237) As *(106)*, I, ix, 9, p. 49

(238) As *(13)*, VIII, 2

(239) As *(9)*, p. 22

(240) As *(235)*

(241) As *(106)*, I, ix, 4ff., p. 48

(242) As *(14)*, II, ii, 7

(243) As *(13)*, VI, i, 8; VIII, 1; VIII, 12

(244) As *(14)*, II, ii, 1

(245) As *(14)*, II, ii, 13–15

(246) As *(85)*, p. 177

(247) Johann Adolf Scheibe, in Friedrich Wilhelm Marpurg, *Kritische Briefe über die Tonkunst,* 3 Vols., Berlin, 1760–4 (issued weekly, 1759–63), for 1760–2

(248) Johann Friedrich Agricola, *Anleitung zur Singkunst,* Berlin, 1757 (actually a German trans., but with very extensive commentaries and additions, including musical examples, of Tosi as at *(20)* above), p. 154

(249) As *(13)*, VIII, 5–6

(250) As *(36)*, IX, 17

(251) As *(106)*, I, ix, 4, p. 48

(252) As *(11)*

(253) As *(14)*, II, v, 3

(254) As *(11)*

(255) Vincenzo Manfredini, *Regole armoniche . . . ,* Venice, 1775, p. 62

(256) As *(149)*, Sect. 8

(257) Girolamo Diruta, *Il Transilvano. Dialogo sopra il vero modo di sonar organi, & istromenti da penna,* Venice, I, 1593, II, 1609 on title-page (presumably publication was delayed, since the dedication is dated 25 March, subsequently to old-style Venetian New Year's day, i.e. 1 March: thus actually 1610): II, iv, 18

(258) As *(69)*, 6

(259) Johann Andreas Herbst, *Musica practica sive instructio pro symphoniacis,* Nuremberg, 1642; 2nd ed. as *Musica moderna prattica . . . ,* Frankfurt, 1653, p. 59

(260) As *(152)*

(261) As *(153)*, p. 164

(262) As *(71)*, [a] p. 76; [b] p. 77; [c] p. 78; [d] p. 83

(263) Randle Cotgrave, compiler, *A Dictionarie of the French and English Tongues,* London, 1611

(264) As *(13)*, XI, 12

(265) Le Sieur Danoville, *L'Art de toucher le dessus et basse de violle,* Paris, 1687, p. 39

(266) As *(32)*, pp. 70ff.

(267) As *(41)*, under TRILLO

(268) As *(160)*, pp. 11ff., 18. Also as *(172)*, p. 13

(269) François Couperin, *Pièces de clavecin, Premier livre,* Paris, 1713, note with the table of ornaments; and as *(9)*, p. 23

(270) *The Compleat Musick-Master,* preface by T[homas] B[rown], London, 1704 (but only known copy is 3rd ed., 1722), Ch. III

(271) As *(163)*, [a] p. 25; [b] p. 28

(272) As *(20)*

(273) As *(248)*

(274) As *(13)*, [a] IX, i; [b] IX, 2; [c] IX, 3; [d] IX, 5; [e] IX, 7; [f] IX, 8; [g] IX, 7

(275) As *(14)*, Pt One, [a] II, ii, 9; [b] II, iii, 13; [c] II, iii, 15

(276) As *(36)*, x, 11 and x, 7

(277) As *(106)*, 1, ix, 7, p. 55; and see French ed. as *Principes du clavecin*, Berlin, 1756, pp. 66, 68

(278) As *(9)*, under 'Agrémens'

(279) Le Sieur de Machy, *Pièces de la violle*, Paris, 1685

(280) As *(71)*, p. 87

(281) Georg Muffat, *Apparatus musico-organisticus*, Salzburg, 1690, preface

(282) As *(85)*, Pt 11, Ch. 3, 55

(283) As *(14)*, Pt One, 1753: [a] 11, v, 4; [b] 11, v, 14; [c] 11, v, 9; [d] 11, v, 10; [e] 11, v, 11

(284) As *(71)*, p. 87

(285) As *(160)*, Ch. VIII

(286) As *(85)*, Pt 11, Ch. 3, 56

(287) As *(14)*, 11, v, 6

(288) Lodovico (Grossi da) Viadana, *Cento concerti ecclesiastici*, Venice, 1602, preface, rule 2

(289) As *(220)*, III (1619), Ch. VI, Sect. on Organ, App.

(290) As *(190)*, Ch. XIX, 14; Ch. XX, rule 19 and rule 8

(291) Matthew Locke, *Melothesia: Or Certain General Rules for Playing upon a Continued-Bass*, London, 1673, rule 10

(292) Andreas Werckmeister, *Die nothwendigsten Anmerckungen . . .*, Aschersleben, [1698], Sect. 70

(293) As *(191)*, rule 8

(294) As *(92)*, [a] Ch. III, p. 19; [b] Ch. v, Sect. 21, p. 86; [c] VI, 71; [d] VIII, 120; [e] VIII, 121; [f] VIII, 128; [g] Ch. IX

(295) Francesco Gasparini, *L'armonico pratico al cembalo*, Venice, 1708, Ch. x

(296) Lorenz Mizler, *Musikalische Bibliothek*, Leipzig, I, Pt 4, 1738, p. 48: and see *(214)* above

(297) Johann Friedrich Daube, *General-Bass in drey Accorden*, Leipzig, 1756, Ch. XI, Sect. 12

(298) As *(13)*, XVII, vi, 4; XVIII, vi, 21

(299) As *(14)*, Pt II (1762), esp. Chs XXIX and XXXII; citations from [a] Introd., 27; [b] XXV, 5; [c] XXV, 6; [d] XXV, 18; [e] XXIX, 5; [f] XXIX, 7; [g] XXIX, 25; [h] XXXII, 10; [i] XXIX, 3; [j] XXIX, 4; [k] XXXII, 6; [l] XXXII, 11; [m] XXXII, 3

(300) As *(92)*, Ch. IX, p. 151

(301) Nicolo Pasquali, *Thorough-Bass Made Easy*, Edinburgh, 1757, p. 47

(302) As *(14)*, Pt. II (1762), Ch. XXXVIII, [a] 3; [b] 4; [c] 5; [d] 8

(302a) As *(10)*, 11, i, 54, note dd (p. 674)

(302b) As *(13)*, XVII, vi, 59

(302c) As *(14)*, Part II, XXXVIII, 3

(303) As *(184)*, pp. 3, 6, 8, 9

(304) As *(289)*

(305) [Peter Prelleur], *The Modern Musick-Master*, London, 1730, ed. of 1731, under 'A Dictionary'

(306) François Couperin, *Leçons de ténèbres*, Paris, 1714, preface

(307) As *(14)*, Pt II (1762), Introd., 3–5, 9

(308) D. Delair, *Traité d'accompagnement*, Paris, 1690, p. 21

(309) François Couperin, *Concerts royaux*, Paris, 1722, preface; *Pièces de clavecin, Troisième livre*, Paris, 1722, preface

(310) As *(199)*

(311) Claudio Monteverdi, letter to the Duke of Mantua, 9 June 1610

(312) As *(207)*, p. 108

(313) Ignazio Donati, *Il secondo libro de motetti a voce, sola,* 'Parte per sonare', preface

(314) As *(163)*, p. 14

(315) Joachim Quantz, autobiographical note (1754) in Friedrich Wilhelm Marpurg, *Historisch-kritische Beyträge*, as *(232)*, I, Berlin, 1755, pp. 231–2

(316) Charles Burney, *The Present State of Music in Germany, the Netherlands, and the United Provinces*, 2 Vols, London, 1773, II, pp. 174, 179

(317) Giambattista Mancini, *Pensieri, e riflessioni pratiche sopra il canto figurato*, Vienna, 1774, pp. 85ff.

(318) Jean-Philippe Rameau, *Pièces de clavecin en concerts*, Paris, 1741, Preface

(319) As *(51)*, under 'Arpeggio'

(320) As *(36)*, II, 5–6; v, 12

(321) As *(8)*, p. 415

(322) As *(16)*, II, v, 303

(323) As *(8)*, p. 35

(324) Jean-Laurent de Béthizy, *Exposition de la théorie et de la pratique de la musique*, Paris, 1754, 2nd ed. of 1764, p. 304

(325) As *(16)*, II, v, 260

Further Reading

To read in whole or part the primary sources from which selected quotations appear in this book is to enter upon a study both difficult and rewarding. There are such inevitable obscurities, discrepancies and omissions; yet somehow a picture builds up of the many moods and varying circumstances of that great area of music we call the baroque period.

The list immediately below contains my special recommendations, most of which are now available in modern facsimiles or reprints. This list is arranged by date of publication, in order to give a chronological overview of the material. Place is an equally important factor, and this is also indicated. Full titles and other details will be found in the alphabetical list next following, which includes these and some other primary sources, as well as some secondary sources which for one reason or another I should like to recommend for particular attention.

It must be clearly understood that these are lists selected for further reading, and *are not intended to be comprehensive*, but simply to represent my own initial choice from the very wide and valuable range of literature available. A very much more extensive but still Select Bibliography will be found in my *Interpretation of Early Music, New Version*, London, 1974, where I included everything known to me and judged by me to be of sufficient relevance and value at the time of going to press. An excellent survey which is not selective, but which is with rare exceptions both reliable and inclusive, is the 'Bibliography of Performance Practices' begun under the editorship of Mary Vinquist and others in *Current Musicology*, No. 8 (1969) with supplements in later issues, and also in book form, edited by Mary Vinquist and Neal Zaslaw, as *Performance Practice: a Bibliography*, New York, 1971.

For keeping up with the latest publications, *Journal of the American Musicological Society*, *Notes* (the Journal of the American Music Library Association, USA), *Music and Letters*, *Musical Times* and *Musical Quarterly* will be found particularly useful. *Early Music* is an invaluable periodical for its excellent reviewing and many articles and illustrations directly relevant to the performance of baroque and other music.

An indispensable tool (though again, of course, not quite infallible) for any advanced work on the primary sources is RISM (*Répertoire international des sources musicales*, B VI: *Écrits imprimés concernant la musique*, ed. F. Lesure, 2 Vols., Munich-Duisberg, 1971). No human product can be quite infallible; that is why the ultimate recourse always needs to be the source itself, or at the very least a good facsimile. But the value of RISM both as a provider of information and as a guide to further research is indeed outstanding, indicating as it does not only the contents of the original title-pages but also the locations and libraries where copies exist.

Some primary sources
arranged by date

(For bibliographical details, see Short List below)

Ganassi, *Fontegara*, Venice, 1535, and *Regola Rubertina*, Venice, 1642–3
Ortiz, *Trattado*, Rome, 1553
Finck, *Practica musica*, Wittenberg, 1556
Zarlino, *Istitutioni*, Venice, 1558
Maffei, *Delle lettere* . . . [letter on voice-production], Naples, 1562
Zacconi, *Prattica di musica*, Venice, 1592–1622
Diruta, *Il Transilvano*, Venice, 1593–1610
Morley, *Plaine and Easie Introduction*, London, 1597
Caccini, *Nuove Musiche*, Florence, 1602
Agazzari, *Del sonare sopra 'l basso*, Siena, 1607
Frescobaldi, *Toccate* [for the famous preface], Rome 1615/16
Praetorius, *Syntagma*, II, Wolfenbüttel, 1618/19
Giustiniani, *Discorso*, [1628]
Mersenne, *Harmonie universelle*, Paris, 1636–7
Kircher, *Musurgia universalis*, Rome, 1650
Playford, *Introduction*, London, 1654, and eds to 1730
Simpson, *Compendium*, London, 1665 etc.
Bacilly, *L'art de bien chanter*, Paris, 1668
Mace, *Musick's Monument*, London, 1676
Jean Rousseau, *Methode claire* . . . *à chanter*, Paris, 1678, and *Traité de la viole*, Paris, 1687
L'Affilard, *Principes tres-faciles*, Paris, 1694
Georg Muffat, *Florilegium primum*, Augsburg, 1695, and *Florilegium secundum*, Passau, 1698 [for the prefaces]
Loulié, *Elements*, Paris, 1696
Roger North, notes and autobiography [London, around 1700]
Brossard, *Dictionaire*, Paris, 1701/3
Raguenet, *Paralele*, Paris, 1702
Saint-Lambert, *Principes du clavecin*, Paris, 1702, and *Nouveau traité de l'accompagnement*, Paris, 1707

Hotteterre, *Principes de la flute traversiere*, Paris, 1707

Gasparini, *L'armonico pratico al cembalo*, Venice, 1708

Couperin, *L'Art de toucher le clavecin*, Paris, 1716/17

Tosi, *Opinioni*, Bologna, 1723

Heinichen, *General-Bass*, Dresden, 1728

Mattheson, *Grosse General-Bass-Schule*, Hamburg, 1731, and *Der Vollkommene Capellmeister*, Hamburg, 1739

Walther, *Musicalisches Lexicon*, Leipzig, 1732

Geminiani, *The Art of Playing on the Violin*, London, 1751

Quantz, *Versuch . . . die Flöte traversiere* [ostensibly a manual for the flute, but actually a general treatise in addition], Berlin, 1752

C. P. E. Bach, *Versuch über . . . das Clavier*, I, Berlin, 1753, II, Berlin, 1762

Marpurg, *Anleitung zum Clavierspielen*, Berlin, 1755

Leopold Mozart, *Violinschule*, Augsburg, 1756

Pasquali, *Thorough-Bass Made Easy*, Edinburgh, 1757

Tartini, *Letter* [dated Padua, 5 March 1760, with hints mainly on bowing techniques]

Jean-Jacques Rousseau, *Dictionnaire de musique*, Paris, 1768, also Amsterdam, 1768

Türk, *Klavierschule*, Leipzig and Halle, 1787

Short list of primary and secondary sources

alphabetically arranged

Aaron [Aron], Pietro, *Thoscanello de la musica*, Venice, 1523

Adlung, Jacob, *Anleitung zu der musikalischen Gelahrheit*, Erfurt, 1758

Agazzari, Agostino, *Del sonare sopra 'l basso con tutti li stromenti e dell'uso loro nel conserto*, Siena, 1607 (esp. for early 17th-cent. orchestration)

Agricola, Johann Friedrich, *Anleitung zur Singkunst*, Berlin, 1757 (Tosi translated with important commentaries)

Alembert, Jean le Rond d', *Élémens de musique, théorique et pratique*, Paris, 1752

Allaire, Gaston G., *The Theory of Hexachords, Solmization and the Modal System*, [n.p.], 1972

Arbeau, Thoinot [Jehan Tabouret], *Orchésographie*, Langres, 1589 (dances)

Arnold, Frank T., *The Art of Accompaniment from a Thorough-Bass as Practised in the XVIIth and XVIIIth Centuries*, London, 1931 (a classic: see the repr. introd. D. Stevens, 2 Vols., New York, 1931)

Auda, Antoine, *Theorie et pratique du tactus: Transcription et exécution de la musique antérieure aux environs de 1650*, Brussels, 1965

Avison, Charles, *An Essay on Musical Expression*, London, 1752

Bach, Carl Philipp Emanuel, *Versuch über die wahre Art das Clavier zu spielen*, Berlin, 1753, Pt. II, Berlin, 1762 (indispensable for the late baroque)

Bacilly, Bénigne de, *Remarques curieuses sur l'art de bien chanter*, Paris, 1668

Badura-Skoda, Eva: *see under* Horsley

Bang, Betty: *see* Mather

Bent, Margaret, Lewis Lockwood, Robert Donington, Stanley Boorman, 'Musica Ficta' in *The New Grove*, London, 1980, Vol. 12, pp. 802–811

Bérard, Jean-Baptiste (or Jean-Antoine), *L'art du chant*, 1755 (authorship disputed by the Abbé Joseph Blanchet, who pub. 2nd ed. under his own name, Paris, 1756)

Berardi, Angelo, *Ragionamenti musicali*, Bologna, 1689

Béthizy, Jean-Laurent de, *Exposition de la théorie et de la pratique de la musique*, Paris, 1754

Bononcini, Giovanni Maria, *Musico prattico*, Bologna, 1673

Boorman, Stanley: *see under* Bent

[Bottrigari, Ercole], *Il Desiderio overo, De' concerti di varij strumenti musicali*, Venice, 1594 (see Carol MacClintock's trans. and ed. of the 1599 ed., [Rome], 1962)

Bovicelli, Giovanni Battista, *Regole, passaggi di musica, madrigali, e motetti passeggiati*, Venice, 1594

Boyden, David D., *The History of Violin Playing from Its Origins to 1761 and Its Relationship to the Violin and Violin Music*, London, 1965 (invaluable)

Brossard, Sébastien de, *Dictionnaire des termes*, Paris, 1701 [but chiefly known in the enl. ed. as] *Dictionaire de musique*, Paris, 1703

Brown, Howard Mayer, *Embellishing 16th-century Music*, London, 1976 (brief but excellent)

Sixteenth-Century Instrumentation: The Music for the Florentine Intermedii, [Rome], 1973 (a detailed monograph but of great general interest)

'Editing', in *The New Grove*, London, 1980, Vol. 5, pp. 839–48

'Performing Practice', in *The New Grove*, London, 1980, Vol. 14, pp. 370–1 and 375–93 (pp. 371–5 have James W. McKinnon on medieval monophony. An excellent entry throughout)

Buelow, George, *Thorough-Bass Accompaniment According to Johann David Heinichen*, Berkeley and Los Angeles, 1966 (includes partial translation and excellent discussion)

Butler, Charles, *The Principles of Musik, in Singing and Setting*, London, 1636 (uses phonetic script)

Caccini, Giulio, *Le nuove musiche*, Florence, 1602 (title-page has 1601, ?Florentine Old Style for pre-March 25, i.e. 1602 modern style; but even so erroneously, since printing was delayed and cannot have occurred before 1 July 1602, the date as finally appended to the imprimatur. End p. has 1602, visibly altered from 1601. Best consulted in the excellent ed. by H. Wiley Hitchcock, Madison, 1970)

Caroso, Fabritio, *Nobiltà di dame*, Venice, 1600 (dances)

Casa, Girolamo dalla, *Il vero modo di diminuir*, 2 Bks, Venice, 1584

Chew, Geoffrey, 'Notation', III, 4, in *The New Grove*, London, 1980, Vol. 13, pp. 373–420 (magnificent; *see also* pp. 333ff.)

[Choquel, Henri Louis] *La musique rendue sensible par la méchanique, ou Nouveau systeme pour apprendre facilement la musique soi-même*, Paris, 1759

Coclico, Adrianus Petit, *Compendium musices*, Nuremberg, 1552

Collins, Michael: *see under* Horsley

Conforti, Giovanni Luca, *Breve et facile maniera d'essercitarsi . . . a far passaggi*, Rome, 1593 [? 1603 – date is blurred]

Couperin, François, *L'Art de toucher le clavecin*, Paris, 1716 [enl. ed.] Paris, 1717 (not so clear as could be wished, but important)

Dadelsen, Georg von, 'Verzierung', *Die Musik in Geschichte und Gegenwart* (MGG), XIII (1966), cols. 1526–56

Dahlaus, Carl, 'Zur Entstehung des modernen Taktsystems im 17. Jahrhundert', *Archiv für Musikwissenschaft*, XVIII (1961), pp. 223–40

Descartes, René, *Musicae compendium* [1618], Utrecht, 1650

Diruta, Girolamo, *Il Transilvano. Dialogo sopra il vero modo di sonar organi, & istromenti da penna*, Venice, 1593; Pt. II, Venice, 1610

Dolmetsch, Arnold, *The Interpretation of the Music of the XVIIth and XVIIIth Centuries Revealed by Contemporary Evidence*, London [1915]

Donington, Robert, *The Interpretation of Early Music*, London, 1963 [but should now be consulted in the much longer and greatly revised] *The Interpretation of Early Music, New Version*, London, 1974

    A Performer's Guide to Baroque Music, London, 1973 (shares some material in common with the longer *Interpretation of Early Music* cited above, but on certain aspects, notably bel canto voice-production and accidentals, is more extensive; and it is in fact a different book which in most respects is condensed to a somewhat shorter scale)

    see also under Bent

Eppelsheim, Jürgen, *Das Orchester in den Werken Jean-Baptiste Lullys*, Tutzing, 1961

Fallows, David, 'Tempo and Expression Marks', in *The New Grove*, London, 1980, Vol. 18, pp. 677–84.

Ferand, Ernest T., *Die Improvisation in der Musik*, Zurich, 1938 (very thorough discussion)

    Die Improvisation in Beispielen aus neun Jahrhunderten abendländischer Musik, Cologne, 1956 [in the series *Das Musikwerk*; also Eng. ed. in the *Anthology of Music*, Cologne, 1961] (music examples)

Finck, Hermann, *Practica musica*, Wittenberg, 1556

Frescobaldi, Girolamo, *Toccate e partite d'intavolatura di cimbalo . . . Libro primo*, Rome, 1615: [2nd ed.] Rome, 1615–16 [with title-page dated 1615, preface engraved 1616] (for the important prefaces)

Fuller, David, 'Notes Inégales', in *The New Grove*, London, 1980, Vol. 13, pp. 420–7 (the best up-to-date account)

Ganassi, Sylvestro di, *Opera intitulata Fontegara, la quale insegna a sonare di flauto*, Venice, 1535

    Regola Rubertina. Regola che insegna. Sonar de viola darcho tastada, Venice, 1542; Pt. II as *Lettione seconda pur della prattica di sonare il violone d'arco da tasti*, Venice, 1543

Gasparini, Francesco, *L'armonico pratico al cimbalo*, Venice, 1708 (particularly valuable for continuo accompanists, who are recommended to the trans. by F. S. Stillings, ed. D. L. Burrows, New Haven, 1963)

Geminiani, Francesco, *The Art of Playing on the Violin*, London, 1751 (see the facs. ed. with good introd. by David D. Boyden, London [1952])

[Giustiniani, Vincenzo] 'Discorso sopra la musica', [1628], trans. and ed. Carol MacClintock, [Rome], 1962

Grassineau, James, *A Musical Dictionary*, London, 1740 (mainly but not wholly pirated from Brossard's *Dictionaire*)

Grove, *The New* (i.e. the 6th ed. of *Grove's Dictionary of Music and Musicians*): *see under* Sadie

Harich-Schneider, Eta, *The Harpsichord: An Introduction to Technique, Style and the Historical Sources*, Kassel and St Louis, 1954 (useful)
   Die Kunst des Cembalo-Spiels, Kassel, 1939; 2nd ed. 1958 (full and excellent)

Heinichen, Johann David, *Der General-Bass in der Composition*, Dresden, 1728 (greatly expanded from his *Anweisung . . . des General-Basses* of Hamburg, 1711: *see also under* Buelow)

Hermann-Bengen, Irmgard, *Tempobezeichnungen: Ursprung, Wandel im 17. und 18. Jahrhundert*, Tutzing, 1959

Horsley, Imogene, Michael Collins, Eva Badura-Skoda, Dennis Libby, 'Improvisation: I, Western Art Music', in *The New Grove*, London, 1980, Vol. 9, pp. 31–52

Hotteterre le Roman [Jacques Martin], *Principes de la flute traversiere, ou flute d'Allemagne; de la flute à bec, ou flute douce, et du haut-bois*, Paris, 1707

Keller, Hermann, *Phrasierung und Artikulation*, Kassel and Basel, 1955

Kircher, Athanasius, *Musurgia universalis*, 2 Vols., Rome, 1650

Kolneder, Walter, *Aufführungspraxis bei Vivaldi*, Leipzig, 1955
   Georg Muffat zur Aufführungspraxis, Strasbourg and Baden-Baden, 1970

L'Affilard, Michel, *Principes tres-faciles pour bien apprendre la musique*, Paris, 1694

Lasocki, David: *see under* Mather

Le Cerf de la Viéville, Jean-Laurent, Seigneur de Freneuse, *Comparaison de la musique italienne et de la musique françoise*, 3 pts., Brussels, 1704–6 (repr. as vols. 2–4 of Jacques Bonnet's *Histoire de la musique*, Amsterdam, [?1721], 1725 and 1726 eds.)

Libby, Dennis: *see under* Horsley

Locke, Matthew, *Melothesia: Or Certain General Rules for Playing upon a Continued-Bass*, London, 1673

Lockwood, Lewis: *see under* Bent

Loulié, Étienne, *Elements ou principes de musique*, Paris, 1696

MacClintock, Carol, ed. and trans., *Readings in the History of Music in Performance*, Bloomington, Indiana, and London, 1979 (most valuable to students)

Mace, Thomas, *Musick's Monument*, London, 1676

McKinnon, James W.: *see under* Brown, 'Performing Practice'

Maffei, Giovanni Camillo, *Delle lettere . . . v'è un discorso della voce*,
    comp. Don Valerio de' Paolo (Naples, 1562), Bk. 1, pp. 5–81, letter 1,
    to Count d'Altavilla (see ed. in N. Bridgman, 'Giovanni Camillo
    Maffei et sa lettre sur le chant', *Revue de musicologie*, XXXVIII, July
    1956, pp. 10–34)

Malcolm, Alexander, *A Treatise of Musick, Speculative, Practical, and
    Historical*, Edinburgh, 1721

Mancini, Giambattista, *Pensieri, e riflessione pratiche sopra il canto
    figurato*, Vienna, 1774

Marpurg, Friedrich Wilhelm, *Anleitung zum Clavierspielen*, Berlin, 1755
    (Fr. ed. as *Principes du clavecin*, Berlin, 1756)

Masson, Charles, *Nouveau traité des regles de la composition de la
    musique*, Paris, 1697

Mather, Betty Bang, *Interpretation of French Music from 1675 to 1775: For
    Woodwind and Other Performers: Additional Comments on German
    and Italian Music*, New York, 1973

Mather, Betty Bang and David Lasocki, *Free Ornamentation in Woodwind
    Music, 1700–1775: An Anthology with Introduction*, New York, 1976
    The Classical Woodwind Cadenza, New York, 1978

Mattheson, Johann, *Grosse General-Bass-Schule*, Hamburg, 1731 (the enl.
    2nd ed. of *Exemplarische Organisten-Probe . . .* , Hamburg, 1719)
    Der neu-eröffnete Orchestre, Hamburg, 1713
    Der vollkommene Capellmeister, Hamburg, 1739

Maugars, André, *Response faite à un curieux sur le sentiment de la musique
    d'Italie. Escrite a Rome le premier octobre 1639*, [?Paris, 1639 or 1640]

Mendel, Arthur, 'Pitch in the 16th and 17th Centuries', *Musical Quarterly*,
    XXXIV, 1948, Jan. pp. 28–45, Apr. pp. 199–221, July pp. 336–57, Oct.
    pp. 575–93, and 'On the Pitches in Use in Bach's Time', *Musical
    Quarterly*, XLI, 1955, July pp. 332–55, Oct. pp. 446–80 [also in A. J.
    Ellis and A. Mendel, *Studies in the History of Musical Pitch*, Amster-
    dam 1968] (a classic study now freshly taken up with radical expan-
    sion and reconsideration in the following entry)
    'Pitch in Western Music since 1500: A Re-examination', *Acta Musicolo-
    gica*, L, 1978, Fasc. 1/11, pp. 1–73 (now comprises the standard
    treatment, and is indispensable)

Mersenne, Marin, *Harmonie universelle*, 2 Pts., Paris, 1636–7 (this confus-
    ingly arranged but essential work is most conveniently approached by
    way of the books on instruments trans. R. E. Chapman, The Hague,
    1957)

Millet, Jean, *La belle méthode, ou l'art de bien chanter*, Lyon, 1666, facs.,
    introd. by A. Cohen, New York, 1973

Morley, Thomas, *A Plaine and Easie Introduction to Practicall Musicke*,
    London, 1597

Mozart, J. G. Leopold, *Versuch einer gründlichen Violinschule*, Augsburg,
    1756 (in effect based upon and in part derived from Tartini, and for us
    an essential document: *see also under* Tartini)

Muffat, Georg, *Suavioris harmoniae instrumentalis hyporchematicae Flori-
    legium primum*, Augsburg, 1695; *. . . Florilegium secundum*, Passau,
    1698 (for important prefaces in multiple languages)

M[ylius], W[olfgang] M[ichael], *Rudimenta musices . . . Anweisung zur Singe-Kunst*, [Gotha], 1685 (but most surviving copies, Gotha, 1686)

Neumann, Frederick, *Ornamentation in Baroque and Post-Baroque Music, with Special Emphasis on J. S. Bach*, Princeton, 1978. A very compulsive and tendentious scholar who does not get all the simpler issues straight, but has gone farther than anyone into the remoter complications, on which this book is indispensable

'The Overdotting Syndrome: Anatomy of a Delusion', *Musical Quarterly*, LXVII, 1981, pp. 305–47 (a lawyer's argument discounting valid evidence to the contrary)

North, Roger, *The Autobiography of Roger North* [c.1695], ed. A. Jessopp, London, 1877; also numerous confused and overlapping MS notes, Brit. Lib., London, esp. Add. 32,537, foll. 66–109 (Essay on Sound, Harmony and 'Aire', c.1710); Add. 32,536, foll. 1–90 ('An Essay of Musicall Ayre', c.1715–20); Add. 32,533, foll. 1–181 ('The Musical Gramarian', c.1726, extract ed. H. Andrews, London, 1925); the whole best approached through John Wilson, trans. and ed., *Roger North on Music: Being a Selection from His Essays Written during the Years c.1695–1728*, London, 1959

Ortiz, Diego, *Trattado de glosas sobre clausulas y otros generos de puntos en la musica de violones*, Rome, 1553

Pasquali, Nicolo, *Thorough-Bass Made Easy*. Edinburgh, 1757

Playford, John, *A Breefe Introduction to the Skill of Musick for Song and Violl*, London, 1654 (19 numbered and several unnumbered eds. with varying titles and contents to 1730)

Praetorius, Michael, *Syntagma musicum*, 3 vols. Wittenberg and Wolfenbüttel, 1614–20 (but most surviving copies 1615–20)

Quantz, Joachim, *Versuch einer Anweisung die Flöte traversiere zu spielen*, Berlin, 1752. Fr. ed.: *Essai d'une methode pour apprendre à jouer de la flute traversiere*, Berlin, 1752 [authorized by Quantz in the preface]. (A true flute-player's manual, but still more a broad treatise on performance generally, and a main source of information for the late baroque.)

[Raguenet, l'abbé François] *Paralele des italiens et des françois, en ce qui regarde la musique et les opéra*, Paris, 1702 [misprinted as 1602] (the trans. as *A Comparison between the French and Italian Musick and Opera's*, London, 1709, was 'conjectured' by Sir John Hawkins to be by J. E. Galliard; disputed by Dr Burney; not proved nor disproved)

Rameau, Jean-Philippe, *Code de musique pratique . . . pour former la voix & l'oreille, pour la position de la main . . . sur le clavecin & l'orgue, pour l'accompagnement*, Paris, 1760

Répertoire international des sources musicales (RISM), B VI: *Écrits imprimés concernant la musique*, ed. F. Lesure, 2 vols., Munich-Duisburg, 1971 (invaluable for looking up bibliographical details and locating copies)

Rose, Gloria, 'Agazzari and the Improvising Orchestra', *Journal of the American Musicological Society (JAMS)*, XVIII, Fall 1965, pp. 382–93

Rousseau, Jean, *Methode claire, certaine et facile, pour apprendre à chanter la musique*, Paris, 1678
  Traité de la viole, Paris, 1687
Rousseau, Jean-Jacques, *Dictionnaire de musique*, Paris, 1768 [Preface, 20 Dec. 1764, Approbation, 15 April 1765, Privilege 30 July 1765; pre-publication copies have been reported, but no earlier eds. confirmed]; also Amsterdam, 1768
Sabatini, Galeazzo, *Regola facile, e breve per sonare sopra il basso continuo*, Venice, 1628
Sadie, Stanley, ed., *The New Grove Dictionary of Music and Musicians*, 20 Vols, London, 1980 (now pre-eminent of its kind)
Saint-Lambert, Michel de, *Nouveau traité de l'accompagnement*, Paris, 1707
  Les principes du clavecin, Paris, 1702
Santa Maria, Fray Tomás de, *Libro llamado Arte de tañer fantasia, assi para tecla como para vihuela*, Valladolid, 1565
Schmitz, Hans-Peter, *Die Kunst der Verzierung im 18. Jahrhundert*, Kassel, 1955; 2nd ed. 1965 (good preface and examples)
Schott, Howard, *Playing the Harpsichord*, London, 1971 (very musicianly and practical)
Simpson, Christopher, *The Division-Violist: or, an Introduction to the Playing upon a Ground*, London, 1659 (2nd ed. as *Chelys . . . The Division-Viol*, 1665)
  The Principles of Practical Musick, London, 1665 (later eds. as *A Compendium . . .*)
Strunk, Oliver, *Source Readings in Music History*, New York, 1950 (long and well-selected extracts)
Tans'ur, William, *A New Musical Grammar*, London, 1746
Tartini, Giuseppe, *Traité des agrémens de la musique* [survives in two Ital. MSS, and dates from before 1756, when L. Mozart drew on it for his *Violonschule*]. Fr. trans. P. Denis, Paris [1771]: ed. Erwin R. Jacobi, with Eng. trans. C. Girdlestone, and facs. of orig. Ital. text, Celle and New York, 1961
Tosi, Pier Francesco, *Opinioni de' cantori antichi, e moderni*, Bologna, 1723. Eng. trans. and ed., J. E. Galliard, as *Observations on the Florid Song*, London, 1742: *see also* Agricola
[Treiber, Johann Philipp] *Der accurate Organist im General-Bass*, Jena, 1704
Türk, Daniel Gottlob, *Klavierschule, oder Anweisung zum Klavierspielen für Lehrer und Lerende*, Leipzig and Halle, 1789 (outstanding in this period)
Viadana, Lodovico (Grossi da), *Cento concerti ecclesiastici*, Venice, 1602 (beginnings of figured bass)
Vinquist, Mary and others, eds., 'Bibliography of Performance Practices', *Current Musicology* No. 8 (1959) and subsequent numbers; also as *Performance Practice: A Bibliography*, ed. M. Vinquist and N. Zaslaw, New York, 1971
Walther, Johann Gottfried, *Musicalisches Lexicon*, Leipzig, 1732
Werckmeister, Andreas, *Die nothwendigsten Anmerckungen, und Regeln*

wie der Bassus continuus, oder General-Bass wol könne tractiret werden, Aschersleben [1698]

Williams, Peter, *Figured Bass Accompaniment*, 2 vols., Edinburgh, 1970. 'Continuo' in *The New Grove*, London, 1980, Vol. 4, pp. 685–99

Wolf, R. Peter, 'Metrical Relationships in French Recitative . . .', *Recherches sur la Musique Française Classique*, Vol. 18, 1978, pp. 29–49 (important)

Zacconi, Lodovico, *Prattica di musica*, Venice, 1592, Pt. II, Venice, 1622

Zarlino, Gioseffo, *Le istitutioni harmoniche*, Venice, 1558 (Vol. 1 of *De tutte l'opere*, Venice, 1589)

Zaslaw, Neal A. 'Materials for the Life and Works of Jean-Marie Leclair l'ainé', Ph.D. diss., Columbia Univ., 1970 (very thorough on late baroque French dance tempos). *See also under* Vinquist

---

Neumann, Frederick, *Essays in Performance Practice*, Ann Arbor, 1982

Index

Index prepared by
David Matthews

*Page numbers in italics indicate quotations,
those in bold type denote more important references.
Musical examples are shown within brackets.*